# Michael Jackson

## Biography

The Pinnacle Portrait of Music

# CONTENT

Chapter 1: Just Kids With a Dream

Chapter 2: The Dream Land

Chapter 3: Dancing Machine

Chapter 4: Me And Q

Chapter 5: The Moonwalk

Chapter 6: All You Need Is Love

# Chapter 1: Just Kids With a Dream

I was born on a late summer night in 1958 in Gary, Indiana, the seventh of my parents' nine children. My father, Joe Jackson, was born in Arkansas and married Katherine Scruse, whose ancestors were from Alabama, in 1949. Maureen, my younger sister, was born the next year and had the difficult task of being the oldest. Next in line were Jackie, Tito, Jermaine, LaToya, and Marlon. Randy and Janet pursued me.

My father's job in the steel factory is one of my first memories. It was a difficult, mind-numbing job, and he used music as an escape. My mother was working in a retail store at the same time. We listened to music all the time at home because of my father and my mother's love of it. My father and his brother were members of the Falcons, a local R&B band. My father and his brother both played the guitar. They would perform classic early rock 'n' roll and blues tunes by Chuck Berry, Little Richard, Otis Redding, and others. All of those genres were incredible, and each had an impact on Joe and us, even if we were too young to realise it at the time. The Falcons practised in our living room in Gary, so I grew up listening to R&B. We were a large family because we had nine kids and my father's brother had eight of his own. We entertained ourselves with music, and those times helped to keep us together and inspired my father to be a family-oriented man. The Jackson 5 were born out of this history—we later became the Jacksons—and because of this training and musical tradition, I was able to go out on my own and create my own sound.

Even though I loved to sing, I recall my childhood as largely work. Unlike Judy Garland, I was not coerced into a career in show business by my parents. I did it because I enjoyed it and it felt as natural to me as breathing in and exhaling. I did it because I felt pushed to do so, not by my parents or family, but by my own inner existence in the music world.

When I initially started performing with my brothers, we were dubbed the Jacksons. We'd later be known as the Jackson 5. Even after we departed Motown, we would regain the Jacksons' name.

Since we took over our own careers and began producing our own music, every one of my or the group's albums has been dedicated to our mother, Katherine Jackson. My earliest recollections of mom are her holding me and singing songs like "You Are My Sunshine" and "Cotton Fields." She frequently sang to me and my brothers and sisters. Despite having resided in Indiana for some time, my mother grew up in Alabama, where it was just as typical for black people to be reared with country and western music on the radio as it was to hear spirituals at church. She still likes Willie Nelson. She has always had a lovely voice, and I believe I inherited it from her, as well as from God.

Years later, after we'd left Gary, we appeared on "The Ed Sullivan Show," the live Sunday night variety show that introduced America to the Beatles, Elvis, and Sly and the Family Stone. Mr. Sullivan congratulated and thanked each of us after the show, but I was thinking about what he had said to me before the show. I was walking around backstage like the kid in the Pepsi commercial when I came across Mr. Sullivan. He shook my hand and seemed pleased to see me, but before he let go, he had a special message for me. It was 1970, a year when some of rock's most talented musicians died as a result of drug and alcohol abuse. In the show industry, an older, wiser generation was unprepared to lose its very young. Some people had already said that I reminded them of Frankie Lymon, a brilliant young singer from the 1950s who died in this manner. "Never forget where your talent came from, that your talent is a gift from God," Ed Sullivan may have been thinking of all this when he told me, "Never forget where your talent came from, that your talent is a gift from God."

If children do not receive the affection they require from their parents, they will seek it from someone else and cling to that person, a grandparent, or anyone. With my mother around, we never had to look for anybody else. The lessons Grandma taught us were priceless. Her priorities were kindness, love, and consideration for others. Don't cause harm to others. Never, ever beg. Never, ever freeload. At our house, such were sins. She always wanted us to offer without asking or begging. That's how she is.

I recall a good tale about my mother that exemplifies her character. When I was a kid in Gary, this man came knocking on everyone's door early in the morning. He was bleeding so profusely that you could see where he'd gone in the neighbourhood. He was refused entry. He eventually went to our door and began banging and knocking. Mother immediately allowed him in. Most people would be too scared to do that, but that's my mother. I recall waking up to find blood on our floor. I wish we were all more like Mom.

My first memories of my father are of him returning from the steel factory with a large bag of glazed doughnuts for all of us. My brothers and I could eat a lot back then, and the bag would go in a flash. He used to take us all to the park merry-go-round, but I was so young that I don't remember anything about it.

My father has always been a mystery to me, and he is well aware of this. One of the few things I regret the most is never being able to truly connect with him. He had formed a protective shell around himself over the years, and once he stopped talking about our family company, he found it difficult to relate to us. We'd be all together, and he'd simply exit the room. Even today, he finds it difficult to discuss father-son issues because he is too humiliated. When I see that he is, I am humiliated as well.

What I received from my father was not necessarily God-given, despite the fact that the Bible states that you reap what you sow. Dad phrased it differently when we were younger, but the message was the same: You could have all the skill in the world, but it wouldn't help you if you didn't prepare and plan.

I was old enough by this point to sneak in and watch if I swore not to tell. Mom finally captured them one day, and we were all worried. She chastised the lads but promised not to inform Dad if we were careful. She knew the instrument was keeping them from running with a nasty mob and maybe getting beat up, so she wasn't about to take away anything that kept them within arm's reach.

Of course, something had to give sooner or later, and one day a string broke. My brothers panicked. There wasn't time to get it repaired before Dad arrived home, and furthermore, none of us knew how to go about getting it fixed. My brothers never knew what to do, so they put the guitar back in the closet and prayed frantically that my father would think it broke by itself. Of course, Dad didn't buy that, and he was upset. My sisters advised me to stay out of it and maintain a low profile. I went to investigate after hearing Tito crying after Dad discovered it. Tito was crying on his bed when Dad returned and beckoned for him to get up. Tito was terrified, but my father simply stood there, clutching his treasured guitar. He gave Tito a stern, probing stare and said, "Let me see what you can do."

My brother gathered himself and began to play a few runs he had taught himself. When my father saw how well Tito could play, he understood he'd definitely been training and that Tito and the rest of us didn't treat his beloved guitar like a toy. It became evident to him that what had occurred was purely coincidental. At this point, my mother intervened and expressed her admiration for our musical skills. She informed him that we boys were talented and that he should pay attention to us. She kept pressing for us, and eventually he started listening, and he loved what he heard. Tito, Jackie, and Jermaine began rehearsing in earnest. When I was approximately five years old, Mom told my father that I was an excellent vocalist and could play the bongos. I joined the organisation.

Around that time, my father realised that what was going on in his family was serious. He gradually began to spend less time with the Falcons and more time with us. We'd just woodshed together, and he'd offer us guitar ideas and methods. Marlon and I were too young to play, but we would observe while my father practised with the bigger boys, and we were learning as we watched. When Dad wasn't there, the rule on using Dad's guitar remained in effect, but my brothers relished the opportunity to do so. The music was blaring from the house on Jackson Street. Rebbie and Jackie had received music lessons from their parents when they were little, so they had an excellent foundation. The rest of us had music class and band in Gary schools, but no amount of practising could keep all that enthusiasm in check.

The Falcons were still making money, despite their few appearances, and that extra cash was crucial to us. It was enough to put food on the table for a growing family, but not enough to buy us unnecessary items. Mom was working part-time at Sears, Dad was still working at the mill, and no one went hungry, but I imagine things must have felt hopeless at the time.

Dad was running late one day, and Mom became concerned. When he poked his head through the door, she was ready to give him a piece of her mind, which we boys didn't mind witnessing every now and then just to see if he could take it like he dished it out, but when he poked his head through the door, he had a mischievous look on his face and he was hiding something behind his back. We were all taken aback when he pulled out a shining red guitar that was somewhat smaller than the one in the closet. We were all praying for the old one to come back. But Dad claimed the new guitar belonged to Tito. We crowded around to admire it, while Dad instructed Tito that he had to share it with anyone who wanted to practise. We weren't supposed to show it off at school. This was a significant gift, and that day was a watershed moment for the Jackson family.

Mom was pleased for us, but she knew her husband. She was more aware than we were of his lofty goals and aspirations for us. He'd started talking to her after we'd all gone to bed. He had dreams, and they didn't end with one instrument. We were quickly dealing with equipment rather than just gifts. Jermaine received a bass and an amp. Jackie was given shakers. Our bedroom and living room resembled a music store. I'd occasionally hear When the question of money came up, Mom and Dad fought since all those instruments and accessories meant missing out on a little something we needed each week. Dad, on the other hand, was convincing and didn't miss a beat.

We even have microphones throughout the home. They seemed like a luxury at the time, especially for a woman on a tight budget, but I've come to realise that having those mics in our house wasn't just an attempt to keep up with the Joneses or anyone else in amateur night competitions. They were there to assist us in our preparations. I've seen people at talent events who sounded terrific at home clam up when they went in front of a microphone. Others began screaming their songs as if they didn't need the microphones. They didn't have the benefit that we did, which only experience can provide. I believe that made some people envious since they could tell our competence with the microphones provided us an advantage. If it were true, we had made so many sacrifices—in terms of leisure time, schooling, and friends—that no one could be jealous. We were improving, but we were working like people twice our age.

Dad got a pair of young guys named Johnny Jackson and Randy Rancifer to play trap drums and organ while I was watching my older siblings, including Marlon on the bongo drums. Motown would later claim they were our relatives, but that was merely a marketing ploy to make us appear to be one huge family. We'd evolved into a real band! I was like a sponge, watching everyone and soaking up as much information as I could. When my siblings were rehearsing or performing at charity events or shopping malls, I was completely absorbed. I was most captivated by Jermaine since he was the singer at the time and he was like a big brother to me—Marlon was too young for that. Jermaine was the one who would walk me to kindergarten and pass down his clothes to me. I attempted to mimic him whenever he did something. My brothers and father would laugh when I was successful, but when I started singing, they listened. I was singing in a baby voice and just copying sounds at the time. I was so little that I didn't understand much of the lyrics, but the more I sang, the better I got.

I'd always been good at dancing. I would follow Marlon's motions because Jermaine had the enormous bass to carry, but also because I was only a year older than Marlon. I soon found myself performing most of the singing at home and preparing to perform with my brothers in public. We were all becoming more aware of our individual strengths and shortcomings as members of the group as our rehearsals progressed, and the change in responsibility was occurring naturally.

Our family's house in Gary was small, simply three rooms, but it seemed much larger to me at the time. When you're that young, the entire world appears so vast that a little room can appear four times its actual size. We were all amazed at how small Gary's house was when we returned years later. I remembered it being enormous, yet you could walk out the back door in five steps from the front door. It was really little bigger than a garage, although it felt fine to us youngsters while we lived there. When you're young, you see things from a completely different perspective.

My memories of our school days in Gary are hazy. On the first day of kindergarten, I was dropped off in front of my school, and I definitely remember dreading it. Naturally, I didn't want my mother to abandon me, and I didn't want to be there.

As all children do, I learned to appreciate my teachers, particularly the women. They were always really nice to us, and they adored me. Those professors were amazing; as I was promoted from one grade to the next, they'd all cry, hug me, and tell me how much they hated to see me leave their classes. I adored my professors so much that I would take my mother's jewellery and offer it to them as gifts. They'd be touched, but my mother ultimately discovered it and stopped my generosity with her belongings. That need to offer them something in return for what I was receiving was a reflection of how much I adored them and that school.

I took part in a program in front of the entire school one day while I was in first grade. Everyone in each class had to do something, so I went home and talked to my folks about it. We agreed I should dress in black and white and sing "Climb Ev'ry Mountain" from The Sound of Music. When I finished that song, the reaction in the auditorium took my breath away. The clapping was deafening, and many were smiling and standing. I couldn't believe it when I saw my instructors crying. I had made everyone pleased. It was an incredible sensation. I was also perplexed because I didn't believe I had done anything noteworthy. I was just singing like I did every night at home. When you're performing, you're not aware of how you sound or how you come across. Simply open your mouth and sing.

Dad soon had us ready for talent shows. He was an excellent trainer who invested both money and time in working with us. God bestows talent on people, but our father taught us how to utilise it. I believe we also had a natural talent for show business. We liked performing and gave it everything we had. Every day after school, he'd come home and practise with us. We'd perform for him and he'd give us feedback. If you made a mistake, you were punished, sometimes with a belt, sometimes with a switch. My father was really strict with us. Marlon was the one who always got in trouble. On the other hand, I'd get beaten for stuff that primarily happened outside of rehearsal. Dad would make me so angry and hurt that I'd want to retaliate, just to be hit even more. I'd take a shoe and toss it at him, or I'd fight back with my hands clenched. That's why I got it more than my brothers put together. My father would kill me or tear me apart if I fought back. Even when I was a baby, my mother assured me I'd fight back, but I don't remember that. I do recall running under tables to get away from him, which only made him furious. We had a tumultuous relationship.

The majority of the time, however, we simply practised. We always practised. We'd have time late at night to play games or play with our toys. We might play hide-and-go-seek or jump rope, but that was about it. We spent most of our time working. When my father got home, I remember hurrying into the house with my brothers knowing we'd be in serious trouble if we didn't start rehearsals on time.

My mother was completely supportive throughout. She was the one who initially noticed our skill and proceeded to assist us in reaching our full potential. It's difficult to picture where we would be without her love and sense of humour. She was concerned about our stress and the long hours of rehearsal, but we wanted to be the best we could be and we loved music.

Gary was a big fan of music. We had our own radio stations and nightclubs, and there were plenty of people who wanted to work for them. Dad would go see a local show or sometimes go all the way to Chicago to see someone perform after our Saturday afternoon rehearsals. He was always on the lookout for things that could aid us in the future. He'd return home and tell us what he'd seen and who had done what. He was up to date on everything, whether it was a local theatre running contests we could enter or a Cavalcade of Stars concert with fantastic acts whose outfits or moves we could mimic. On Sundays, I wouldn't see Dad until I got home from Kingdom Hall, but as soon as I walked into the house, he'd be telling me about what he'd witnessed the night before. He'd convince me that if I only tried this step, I'd be able to dance on one leg like James Brown. There I'd be, fresh out of church and back in the spotlight.

When I was six years old, we began collecting trophies for our act. Our lineup was set: I was second from the left, facing the audience, with Jermaine on the wing next to me and Jackie on my right. Tito and his guitar took centre stage, with Marlon close behind. Jackie was growing taller and taller, towering over Marlon and me. We used the same setup for the contest after the event, and it worked great. While other groups we met would quarrel and disband, we were growing more polished and experienced. People in Gary who came to see the talent events on a regular basis got to know us, so we would strive to outdo ourselves and surprise them. We didn't want them to become bored with our performance. We knew that change was always beneficial and that it allowed us to grow, therefore we were never afraid of it.

Winning an amateur night or talent show in a ten-minute, two-song set required the same amount of effort as a ninety-minute concert. I'm certain that because there is no room for error, your focus burns you up inside more on one or two songs than it does on twelve or fifteen in a set. These talent shows served as our professional training. We'd travel hundreds of miles to perform one or two songs, hoping that the crowd wouldn't turn against us because we weren't local talent. We were up against people of various ages and abilities, including drill teams, comedians, and other singers and dancers like us. We needed to capture and hold that audience. Nothing was left to chance, so clothes, shoes, hair, and everything else had to be exactly as Dad had intended. We appeared quite professional. After all of our preparation, if we played the songs as we had practised them, the awards would take care of themselves. This was true even when we were in the Wallace High area, which had its own performers and cheering sections, and we were challenging them directly in their own backyards. Naturally, local performers had their own very loyal followers, so it was difficult to leave our turf and enter someone else's. We wanted to make sure that when the master of ceremonies placed his hand over our heads for the "applause metre," the crowd knew we had donated more than everyone else.

Jermaine, Tito, and the rest of us were under a lot of pressure as players. Our manager was the type who reminded us that if the Famous Flames missed a cue or twisted a note during a performance, James Brown would penalise them. As lead singer, I thought I couldn't afford to have a "off night." I recall being onstage late at night after being sick in bed all day. It was difficult to concentrate at the time, but I knew everything my brothers and I had to accomplish so well that I could have done it in my sleep. I had to tell myself not to glance in the crowd for someone I recognized or at the emcee, both of which might distract a young performer. We performed songs that people had heard on the radio or that my father knew were already classics. If you made a mistake, the audience would know because they understood the songs and how they were intended to sound. If you changed an arrangement, it had to sound better than the original.

When I was eight, we won the citywide talent event with our rendition of the Temptations' "My Girl." The competition was held at Roosevelt High School, which was only a few blocks away. We had folks on their feet for the entire song, from Jermaine's initial bass notes and Tito's first guitar licks to all five of us singing the chorus. While Marlon and Jackie spun like tops, Jermaine and I traded verses. It was a great experience for all of us to pass that trophy, our biggest yet, back and forth. It was eventually held up in the front seat like a newborn, and Dad told us, "When you do it like you did tonight, they can't not give it to you."

We were now Gary city champs, and Chicago was our next destination since it gave the most consistent work and the best word of mouth for miles and miles. We began seriously planning our strategy. My father's band played the Chicago sound of Muddy Waters and Howlin' Wolf, but he was adaptable enough to recognize that the more lively, slicker sounds that appealed to us youngsters had a lot to offer. We were fortunate because some of his peers were not as hip. In fact, we knew musicians who believed the sound of the sixties was beneath people their age, but not Dad. He recognized outstanding singing when he heard it, even telling us that he saw the Spaniels, Gary's great doo-wop group, when they were stars not much older than us. When Smokey Robinson of the Miracles sang a song like "Tracks of My Tears" or "Ooo, Baby Baby," he listened as intently as we did.

Musically, the 1960s did not abandon Chicago. Great vocalists like Curtis Mayfield, Jerry Butler, Major Lance, and Tyrone Davis were performing at the same venues where we were. My father was managing us full-time at this point, with only a part-time shift at the mill. Mom had some reservations about this decision, not because she didn't think we were excellent, but because she didn't know anybody else who spent the most of his time trying to get his children into the music profession. She was even more disappointed when Dad informed her that he had booked us as a regular performance at Mr. Lucky's, a Gary nightclub. We were compelled to spend our weekends in Chicago and other cities competing in an increasing number of amateur shows, and these travels were costly, so the job at Mr. Lucky's was a means to make it all possible. Mom was startled by the reception we were receiving, and while she was delighted with the prizes and attention, she was concerned for us. Because of my age, she was concerned about me. "This is quite a life for a nine-year-old," she'd add, her gaze fixed on my father.

I'm not sure what my brothers and I expected, but the nightclub crowds weren't the same as the crowds at Roosevelt High. We were pitting lousy comedians against cocktail organists and strippers. Mom was worried that because of my Witness upbringing, I was hanging out with the wrong people and learning things that I'd be better off discovering much later in life. She didn't have to be concerned; just looking at any of those strippers wasn't going to get me into trouble—certainly not at nine years old! But that was a terrible way to live, and it made us even more motivated to advance up the circuit and as far away from that existence as we could.

Being at Mr. Lucky's meant we had an entire show to do for the first time in our lives—five sets a night, six nights a week—and if Dad could find us something out of town for the seventh night, he would. We were working hard, but the bar patrons weren't too unpleasant. They liked James Brown and Sam and Dave just as much as we did, and we were a bonus that came with the drinking and partying, so they were surprised and joyful. We even had a little fun with them on one song, Joe Tex's "Skinny Legs and All." We'd start the song, and somewhere in the midst, I'd go out into the audience, crawl under the tables, and pull up the ladies' skirts to see what was going on. People would throw money at me as I ran by, and when I started dancing, I'd sweep up all the dollars and coins that had fallen to the floor and stuff them into the pockets of my jacket.

Because of my previous experience with talent show audiences, I wasn't particularly nervous when we started playing in clubs. I was always up for going out and performing, you know, just doing it—singing and dancing and having a good time.

We worked in several clubs that featured strippers back then. I used to stand in the wings of this one Chicago restaurant and observe a lady named Mary Rose. I was maybe nine or 10 years old. This girl would strip naked and throw her underwear to the audience. The men would pick them up, sniff them, and yell at them. My brothers and I would be observing and absorbing everything, and my father would not mind. We were exposed to a lot while working on that circuit. They had cut a small hole in the musicians' dressing room wall, which also served as a wall in the women' bathroom. You could look through this hole, and I saw things I'll never forget. Guys on the circuit were so wild that they were constantly drilling small holes in the walls of the ladies' restroom. Of course, I'm sure my brothers and I were squabbling over who got to peer through the hole first. "Get outta the way, it's my turn!" We are pushing each other away in order to make room for ourselves.

Later, when we performed at the Apollo Theater in New York, I witnessed something that really astounded me because I had never thought such things existed. I'd seen a lot of strippers, but that night, this one girl with lovely eyelashes and long hair came out and performed her routine. She delivered an outstanding performance. At the end, she removed her wig, withdrew a pair of large oranges from her bra, and revealed that she was a hard-faced guy beneath all that makeup. That blew my mind. I was only a child and couldn't fathom anything like that. But when I looked out at the theatrical crowd, they were all in, applauding and cheering. I'm just a kid standing in the wings, observing all of this insane stuff.

I was astounded.

As I already stated, I was well educated as a child. More than the majority. Perhaps this allowed me to focus on other parts of my adult life.

Dad brought home a tape of music we'd never heard before, not long after we'd been doing well in Chicago clubs. We were used to doing popular songs from the radio, so we were perplexed as to why he began playing these songs over and over again, with just one guy singing poorly and some guitar chords in the background. Dad explained that the man on the cassette wasn't a performer, but rather a songwriter who had a recording studio in Gary. Mr. Keith had given us a week to practise his songs in order to see if we could make a record out of them. We were naturally ecstatic. We were looking to make a record, any record.

We concentrated solely on the sound, skipping the usual dance routines for a new song. It wasn't as much fun to perform a song that none of us knew, but we were already polished enough to disguise our displeasure and give it our all. After a few false starts and more than a few pep talks, Dad got us on camera when we were ready and felt we had done our best with the content. After a few days of trying to figure out whether Mr. Keith liked the cassette we had made for him, Dad arrived out of nowhere with more of his songs for us to practise for our first recording session.

Mr. Keith, like Dad, was a mill worker who enjoyed music, but he was more interested in the recording and business side of things. Steeltown was the name of his studio and label. Looking back, I realise Mr. Keith was just as delighted as the rest of us. We went to his studio downtown one Saturday morning before "The Road Runner Show," my favourite show at the time. Mr. Keith greeted us at the door and welcomed us inside the studio. He showed us a tiny glass booth filled with various pieces of equipment and explained what each one did. We didn't appear to be required to bend over any more tape recorders, at least not in this studio. I put on some large metal headphones that came halfway down my neck and pretended to be ready for anything.

Some backup vocalists and a horn group arrived as my brothers were figuring out where to plug in their instruments and stand. I initially thought they were there to make a record after us. When we discovered they were coming to record with us, we were overjoyed and amazed. We looked across at Dad, but his expression remained unchanged. He'd obviously known about it and given his approval. Even back then, no one dared to surprise Dad. We were told to pay attention to Mr. Keith, who would give us instructions while we were in the booth. If we followed his advice, the record would take care of itself.

We finished Mr. Keith's first song after a few hours. Some of the backup singers and horn players had never made a record before and found it challenging, but they also didn't have a perfectionist for a manager, so they weren't used to performing things over and over. At times like these, we recognized how hard Dad worked to make us into consummate professionals. We returned the following Saturdays, putting the songs we'd practised over the week into the can and taking home a new cassette from Mr. Keith. Dad even brought his guitar in to perform with us one Saturday. It was the only time he had ever recorded with us. Mr. Keith offered us some copies of the records once they were pressed so we could sell them between sets and after gigs. We understood it wasn't how the big groups did it, but everyone had to start somewhere, and having a record with your group's name on it was a significant deal back then. We were quite fortunate.

"Big Boy," the first Steeltown single, had a killer bass line. It was a sweet song about a young boy who wished to fall in love with a female. Of course, you have to visualise a tiny nine-year-old performing this song to get the entire picture. I didn't want to hear fairy tales any longer, but I was much too young to understand the true meanings of most of the words in these songs. I simply sang what they handed me.

We became a big deal in our neighbourhood when that song with its amazing bass line started getting radio play in Gary. Nobody believed we had our own record. It was difficult for us to believe.

After that first Steeltown record, we set our sights on all of Chicago's major talent shows. Because I was so small, the other acts, especially those that came after us, would usually scrutinise me when they met me. Jackie was laughing one day, as if someone had told him the best joke in the world. This wasn't a good indication shortly before a performance, and I could tell Dad was nervous about messing up onstage. Dad approached him to say something, but Jackie whispered something in his ear, and soon Dad was grabbing his sides and giggling. I, too, was curious about the joke. Dad boasted that Jackie had overheard the headline act conversing among themselves. One of the men replied, "We'd better not let those Jackson 5 cut us tonight with that midget they've got."

I was initially upset because my feelings had been damaged. I assumed they were being cruel. I couldn't help myself because I was the shortest, but soon all the other brothers were laughing as well. They weren't laughing at me, according to Dad. He told me I should be proud since the group assumed I was a grown-up disguised as a youngster, like one of the Munchkins in The Wizard of Oz. Dad stated that if I could get those slick guys talking like the neighbourhood kids who used to bother us in Gary, we'd have Chicago on the run.

We still had our own business to handle. Dad booked us up for the Royal Theater amateur night competition in town after we played some very good clubs in Chicago. He went to see B. B. King at the Regal the night before he recorded his renowned live album. Years ago, when Dad gave Tito that brilliant red guitar, we taunted him by thinking of girls he could name his guitar after, such as B. B. King's Lucille.

We won that show three weeks in a row, with a new song every week to keep the regular audience members guessing. Some of the other performers grumbled that we were being greedy by returning, but they were chasing the same thing we were. There was a rule that if you won amateur night three times in a row, you'd be called back to conduct a paid show for thousands of people, not dozens, as we were doing in bars. We got that chance, and the show was headed by Gladys Knight and the Pips, who were debuting a brand-new song called "I Heard It Through the Grapevine." It had been a wild night.

We had one more huge amateur show after Chicago that we thought we needed to win: the Apollo Theater in New York City. A lot of people in Chicago felt a win at the Apollo was just a good luck charm, but Dad saw it as much more. He understood New York, like Chicago, had a high grade of talent, and he knew New York had more record people and professional musicians than Chicago. If we can do it in New York, we can do it anywhere. That's what an Apollo victory meant to us.

Chicago had submitted a scouting report to New York, and our reputation was such that Apollo accepted us in the "Superdog" finals despite the fact that we hadn't participated in any of the preliminary competitions. Gladys Knight had already approached us about coming to Motown, as had Bobby Taylor, a member of the Vancouvers with whom my father had developed a friendship. Dad had told them we'd be pleased to audition for Motown, but that wasn't in the cards for the time being.

We arrived early enough at the Apollo on 125th Street to get a guided tour. We proceeded into the theatre, looking at all of the photos of the stars who had appeared there, both white and black. The manager finished by leading us to the changing room, but by then I'd found photos of all my favourite players.

I carefully watched all the stars while my brothers and I were paying our dues on the so-called "chitlin' circuit," opening for other acts, because I wanted to learn as much as I could. I'd look at their feet, the way they held their arms, the way they grasped a microphone, trying to figure out what they were doing and why. I knew every step, every grunt, every spin and turn after studying James Brown from the wings. I have to admit that he would put on a show that would tire you emotionally. His entire physical presence, the fire bursting from his pores, would be incredible. You'd feel every drop of perspiration on his brow and understand what he was going through. Nobody has ever performed like him. Truly unbelievable. I'd be there when I saw someone I liked. James Brown, Jackie Wilson, Sam and Dave, and the O'Jays were all great crowd pleasers.

I think I learnt more from Jackie Wilson than from anyone or anything else. All of this was a crucial aspect of my schooling.

We'd stand offstage, behind the curtains, and watch everyone leave after performing, all sweaty. I'd just stand there in awe, watching them go past. And they'd all be wearing these stunning patent-leather shoes. My entire fantasy seemed to revolve around having a pair of patent-leather shoes. I recall being devastated because they didn't produce them in small boy sizes. When I went from store to store looking for patent-leather shoes, they'd tell me, "We don't make them that small." I was really disappointed because I wanted shoes that looked like the ones on stage, shiny and gleaming and turning red and orange when the lights struck them. Oh, how I desired patent-leather shoes similar to those worn by Jackie Wilson.

Backstage, I was usually by myself. My brothers would be upstairs eating and conversing, while I sat in the wings, huddled low, clutching the dusty, stinky curtain and watching the spectacle. I mean, I paid attention to every step, every move, every twist, every bend, every grind, every emotion, and every light move. That was both my education and my entertainment. When I had free time, I was always present. My father, brothers, and other musicians all knew where to look for me. They teased me about it, but I was too preoccupied with what I was seeing or recalling what I had just seen to care. I recall all of those theatres: the Regal, the Uptown, and the Apollo, to mention a few. The talent that emerged from those areas is legendary. Observing masters at work is the best education in the world. You couldn't teach someone what I've learnt by simply standing there and watching. Some performers, such as Bruce Springsteen and U2, may believe they received their schooling on the streets. At core, I'm a performer. Mine came from the stage.

Jackie Wilson was on Apollo's wall. The camera caught him with one leg up, twisted but still in place from grabbing the mike stand he'd just whipped back and forth. He could have been singing a sorrowful lyric like "Lonely Teardrops," but his movement had that audience so transfixed that no one could feel sad or lonely.

The photograph of Sam and Dave was down the corridor, next to an old big-band photograph. Dad had been acquainted with Sam Moore. I recall being pleasantly surprised when I met him for the first time. I'd been singing his tunes for so long that I assumed he'd want to punch my ears out. James Brown, "The King of Them All, Mr. Dynamite, Mr. Please Please Himself," was not far away. Before he arrived, a singer was just a vocalist, and a dancer was just a dancer. A singer could sing and a dancer could dance, but unless you were Fred Astaire or Gene Kelly, you usually did one better than the other, especially in a public performance. But he altered everything. When he skidded across the stage, no spotlight could keep up with him—you had to flood it! I aspired to be that talented.

We won the Apollo amateur night competition, and I felt compelled to return to those images on the walls and express my gratitude to my "teachers." Dad was overjoyed and stated that he could have gone back to Gary that night. He and we were on top of the world. My brothers and I had all received consecutive A's and were expecting to skip a "grade." I had a feeling we wouldn't be performing talent shows and strip spots for much longer.

We were introduced to the music of a family group that would revolutionise our sound and our life in the summer of 1968. They didn't all share a surname, they were black and white, men and women, and they were known as Sly and the Family Stone. They had some incredible successes throughout the years, including "Dance to the Music," "Stand," and "Hot Fun in the Summertime." My brothers would point at me when they heard the lyrics about the midget standing tall, and by now I'd laugh along with them. We heard these tunes all over the radio, including rock stations. They had a huge influence on all of us Jacksons, and we owe them so much.

Following Apollo, we continued to play with one eye on the map and one ear to the phone. Mom and Dad had a rule of no more than five minutes per call, but after we returned from the Apollo, even five minutes seemed excessive. We had to keep the lines open in case somebody from a record label needed to contact us. We lived in constant terror that they might get a busy signal. We were hoping to hear from a specific record label, and if they called, we wanted to answer.

While we waited, we discovered that someone who had seen us at the Apollo had suggested we go to "The David Frost Show" in New York City. We were going to be on television! That was the most exciting experience we'd ever had. I told everyone at school, including those who didn't believe me the first time. We planned to drive out there in a few days. I was keeping track of the time. I had anticipated the entire trip, imagining what the studio would be like and what it would be like to look into a television camera.

I returned home with the travelling homework that my teacher had prepared ahead of time. We did one more dress rehearsal before making our final music pick. I was curious about the tunes we'd be performing.

Dad called that afternoon to cancel the trip to New York. We all came to a halt and just gazed at him.

We were taken aback. I was prepared to cry. We were ready to land our big break. How could they be so cruel to us? What was the situation? What had caused Mr. Frost to change his mind? I was reeling, and I believe everyone else was as well. "I cancelled it," said my father calmly. We all stared at him again, unable to speak. "Motown called." A chill ran down my spine.

I recall the days leading up to that trip with remarkable clarity. I can picture myself outside Randy's first-grade classroom. Today was

Marlon's time to walk him home, but we switched.

Randy's teacher wished me luck in Detroit because Randy informed her we were going to audition in Motown. He was so ecstatic that I had to remind myself that he had no idea what Detroit was. Randy had no idea what a city was, and his family had only been talking about Motown. In the classroom, the teacher said he was looking for Motown on the globe. She suggested that we do "You Don't Know Like I Know" the way she saw us do it at the Regal in Chicago when a group of teachers drove over to see us. I assisted Randy in putting on his coat and politely promised to keep it in mind, knowing that we couldn't sing a Sam and Dave song at a Motown audition because they were on a competitor label, Stax. Dad informed us the corporations were serious about that kind of thing, so he wanted us to know there would be no nonsense when we arrived. He glanced at me and said he hoped his ten-year-old vocalist would live to be eleven.

We hurried out of the Garrett Elementary School building for the short walk home. I recall becoming nervous as a car passed by, then another. Randy clasped my hand in his, and the two of us waved at the crossing guard. I knew LaToya would have to go out of her way to take Randy to school the next day because Marlon and I were staying in Detroit with the others.

The last time we played at the Fox Theater in Detroit, we left directly after the show and returned to Gary about five a.m. I slept most of the way there, so getting to school that morning wasn't as horrible as it could have been. But by three o'clock in the afternoon, I was dragging around like someone with lead weights for feet.

We could have departed straight after our set because we were third on the lineup, but we would have missed the headliner, Jackie Wilson. I'd seen him on other stages before, but at the Fox, he and his band were on a rising stage that moved higher as he began his performance. I remember performing some of those techniques in rehearsal after practising in front of a long mirror in the school toilet as the other kids looked on, tired as I was after school the next day. My father was thrilled, and those steps were integrated into one of my routines.

There was a large puddle just before Randy and I turned the corner onto Jackson Street. I checked for cars but couldn't find any, so I let go of Randy's hand and hopped the puddle, catching on my toes so I wouldn't get my corduroy cuffs wet. I returned my gaze to Randy, knowing he wanted to do the same things I did. He took a step back to get a running start, but I noticed it was a really huge puddle, too big for him to cross without getting wet, so I caught him before he landed short and got wet, being a big brother first and a dance teacher second.

The neighbourhood kids were purchasing candy across the street, and even some of the kids who were picking on me at school inquired when we were going to Motown. I told them and used my allowance to buy chocolates for them and Randy. I didn't want Randy to be sad about my departure.

As we approached the house I heard Marlon yell, "Someone shut that door!" The side of our VW minibus was wide open, and I shuddered, thinking about how cold it was going to be on the long ride up to Detroit. Marlon had arrived before us and was already assisting Jackie in loading our belongings onto the bus. For once, Jackie and Tito arrived home on time: they were meant to have basketball practice, but the winter in Indiana had been nothing but slush, and we were eager to get a strong start. Jackie was on the high school basketball team that year, and Dad used to joke that the next time we'd be in Indianapolis, it'd be when Roosevelt won the state title. The Jackson 5 would perform between the evening and morning games, and Jackie would sink the game-winning shot. Dad enjoyed teasing us, but you never knew what would happen with the

Jacksons. He urged us to excel in many areas, not just music. I believe he received that drive from his father, who was a teacher. My professors were never as harsh on us as he was, despite the fact that they were paid to be stern and demanding.

Mom stepped in and handed us the thermos and sandwiches she had packed. I recall Mom urging me not to rip the dress shirt she had brought for me the night before after stitching it up. Randy and I helped load some items onto the bus before returning to the kitchen, where Rebbie had one eye on Dad's meal and the other on tiny Janet, who was in the high chair.

Rebbie's life being the oldest was never easy. We knew that after the Motown audition was finished, we'd find out whether or not we had to relocate. If we did, she and her fiancé would relocate south. She was always in charge when Mom was attending night school to complete the high school certificate she was denied due to her illness. When Mom told us she was going to obtain her diploma, I couldn't believe it. I recall being worried that she'd have to go to school with kids her age, Jackie or Tito, and that they'd mock her. I recall her laughing when I told her this and gently explaining that she'd be with other adults. It was unusual to have a mother who completed homework just like the rest of us.

Loading the bus was less difficult than usual. Normally, Ronnie and Johnny would have joined us, but Motown's own musicians were performing behind us, so we were on our own. When I walked in, Jermaine was finishing up some assignments in our room. I could tell he was eager to get them out of the way. He informed me that since Jackie had taken the driver's ed and had a set of keys, we should go to Motown by ourselves and leave Dad at home. We both chuckled, but I couldn't picture going anywhere without Dad. Even when Mom conducted our after-school rehearsals since Dad hadn't returned home from his shift on time, it felt like he was there because she functioned as his eyes and ears. She was always aware of what had gone well the night before and what had gone wrong today. At night, Dad would pick it up from there. It felt like they were giving each other signals or something—Dad could always know if we were playing properly by some invisible suggestion from Mom.

When we departed for Motown, there was no lingering goodbye at the door. Mom was used to us being gone for days and during school breaks. LaToya pouted slightly because she was eager to leave. She'd only seen us in Chicago, and we'd never been able to stay in places like Boston or Phoenix long enough to bring her anything. Because she had to stay at home and attend school, I imagine our life must have seemed very beautiful to her. Rebbie had her hands full attempting to put Janet to sleep, but she waved and said good-by. I kissed Randy on the cheek goodbye and we were on our way.

Dad and Jackie flipped through the map as we drove away, partly out of habit, because we'd been to Detroit before. As we drove through town, we passed Mr. Keith's recording studio downtown near City Hall. We'd done some demos at Mr. Keith's that Dad had sent to Motown following the Steeltown record. When we got on the highway, the sun was setting. Marlon declared that hearing one of our songs on WVON would bring us good fortune. We were all nodding. As he encouraged Jackie to remain silent, Dad inquired if we knew what WVON stood for. I continued to stare out the window, contemplating the possibilities that lie ahead, until Jermaine interrupted me. "Voice of the Negro," he announced. We were soon dialling numbers all over the place. "WGN—World's Greatest Newspaper." (It was owned by the Chicago Tribune.) "WLS—World's Largest Store." (Sears.) "WCFL ..." We came to a halt, perplexed. "Chicago Federation of Labor," Dad explained as he reached for the thermos. As we approached I-94, the Gary station faded into a Kalamazoo station. We started switching through the channels, looking for Beatles music on CKLW from Windsor, Ontario, Canada.

At home, I had always been a Monopoly enthusiast, and there was something about going to Motown that reminded me of that game. You move around the board in Monopoly buying items and making decisions; the "chitlin' circuit" of theatres where we played and won contests was like a Monopoly board full of possibilities and perils. After all of the stops, we arrived at the Apollo Theater in Harlem, which was unquestionably Park Place for young artists like us. We were now making our way up the Boardwalk toward Motown. Would we win the game or lose with a large board between us and our aim for another round?

Something was changing within me, and I could feel it, while shivering in the minibus. For years, we'd drive to Chicago, wondering whether we'd ever be good enough to get out of Gary, and we were. Then we drove to New York, confident that if we didn't make it there, we'd tumble off the edge of the planet. Even those evenings in Philadelphia and Washington weren't enough to keep me from wondering whether there wasn't someone or some group in New York we didn't know about who could beat us. We finally felt like nothing could stop us when we tore it down at the Apollo. We were going to Motown, and nothing would surprise us there either. We planned to surprise them, like we always did.

Dad took the typewritten directions from the glove compartment and we exited the freeway near the Woodward Avenue exit. Because it being a school night for everyone else, there weren't many people on the streets.

Dad was concerned about our accommodations, which shocked me until I realised the Motown people had chosen the hotel. We weren't used to people doing things for us. We preferred to be our own bosses. Dad had always been our booking, travel, and management agent. Mom was in charge of the arrangements while he wasn't. So it's no surprise that even Motown managed to make Dad suspicious that he should have arranged the arrangements and handled everything.

The Gotham Hotel was where we stayed. Everything was in order because the bookings had been made. There was a TV in our room, but all the channels had gone off the air, and with the audition at ten o'clock, we wouldn't be able to stay up any later. Dad tucked us into bed, locked the door, and left. Jermaine and I were too exhausted to talk.

Dad made sure we were all awake on time the next morning. However, we were just as excited as he was and jumped out of bed when he called. We had not played in many places where people expected us to be professional, so the audition was unique for us. We understood it would be tough to determine how well we were doing. We were used to getting a reaction from the audience, whether we were competing or simply performing at a club, but Dad had informed us that the longer we remained, the more people wanted to hear.

After cereal and milk at the coffee shop, we stepped into the VW. I noticed grits on the menu, so I knew there were a lot of Southerners staying there. We had never travelled to the South before and hoped to visit Mom's home state eventually. We wanted to understand our own and other black people's roots, especially after what happened to Dr. King. I vividly recall the day he died. Everyone was in shambles. We didn't practise that night. I went to Kingdom Hall with Mom and a few other people. People were sobbing as if they had lost a family member. Even the men, who were normally very emotionless, couldn't hold back their tears. I was too young to understand the whole sorrow of the situation, but remembering that day today makes me want to cry—for Dr. King, his family, and all of us.

Jermaine was the first to notice the studio, which was known as Hitsville, United States of America. It appeared to be run-down, which was not what I had imagined. We wondered who we may see, who might be recording that day. Dad had instructed us to allow him to do all of the talking. Our task was to perform as if we'd never done it before. And that was a lot to ask, given we always put our all into each performance, but we understood what he meant.

There were a lot of people inside waiting for us, but as Dad said the password, a man in a suit and tie stepped out to greet us. He knew all of our names, which surprised us. He requested that we leave our coats behind and accompany him. The other folks merely looked at us as if we were ghosts. I was curious about who they were and what their tales were. Had they travelled a long distance? Had they come every day, expecting to get in without an appointment?

When we walked inside the studio, one of the Motown men was fiddling with a movie camera. There was a section with instruments and microphones set up. Dad went into one of the sound booths to speak with someone. I pretended I was at the Fox Theater, on the rising stage, and that everything was normal. Looking around, I determined that if I ever constructed my own studio, I'd acquire a mike like the one at the Apollo, which rose out of the floor. When it slowly slipped beneath the stage floor, I nearly fell on my face while sprinting down the basement steps, attempting to figure out where it went.

The last song we performed was "Who's Lovin' You." No one applauded or said anything when it concluded. I couldn't bear the thought of not knowing, so I blurted out, "How was that?" Jermaine shook his head. The older men who were supporting us were giggling over something. I caught a glimpse of them out of the corner of my eye. "Jackson Jive, huh?" one of them exclaimed, his face lit up. I was perplexed. My brothers, I believe, were as well.

"Thank you for coming up," the man who had led us back stated. We looked at Dad's face for cues, but he didn't appear pleased or disappointed. We departed when it was still light outside. We drove back to Gary on I-94, subdued, knowing we had homework for class tomorrow and wondering whether that was all there was to it.

# Chapter 2: The Dream Land

We were overjoyed to learn that we had passed the Motown audition. Berry Gordy sat us all down and told us that we were going to make history together. "I'm gonna make you the biggest thing in the world," he went on to say, "and you're gonna be written about in history books." That is exactly what he stated to us. "Okay! Okay!" we said, leaning closer and listening to him. That is something I will never forget. We were all over at his place, and hearing this great, creative man tell us we were going to be very large felt like a fairy story come true.

So Diana didn't locate us first, but I don't think we'll ever be able to adequately repay Diana for everything she did for us back then. When we ultimately moved to Southern California, we actually lived with Diana and stayed with her on a part-time basis for more than a year. Others of us lived with Berry Gordy, others with Diana, and then we switched. She was amazing, mothering us and making us feel at ease. She took care of us for at least a year and a half while my parents closed down the Gary house and hunted for a house in California that we could all live in. It was ideal for us because Berry and Diana shared a Beverly Hills street. We may walk up to Berry's house before returning to Diana's. I'd usually spend the day at Diana's and the night at Berry's. Diana liked art and pushed me to appreciate it as well, so this was a pivotal time in my life. She took the time to educate me on the subject. We'd go shopping for pencils and paint virtually every day, just the two of us. We went to museums when we weren't drawing or painting. She introduced me to the works of famous artists such as Michelangelo and Degas, which sparked my lifelong passion in art. She truly did teach me a lot. It was both new and intriguing to me. It was very different from what I was used to, which was living and breathing music and rehearsing every day. You wouldn't imagine a major figure like Diana would take the time to teach a kid to paint and educate him in the arts, but she did, and I admired her for it. I continue to do so. I'm completely smitten by her. She was my mother, lover, and sister all rolled into one incredible individual.

Motown had never recorded a kids' group back then. Stevie Wonder was the only child vocalist they had ever produced. So Motown was adamant that if they were going to promote children, they would encourage children who were talented in areas other than singing and dancing. They wanted people to like us for who we were, not simply for our records. They wanted us to set a good example by completing our schoolwork and being courteous to our fans, reporters, and anybody else who came into contact with us. This was not difficult for us because our mother had raised us to be respectful and considerate. It was automatic. Our main issue with academics was that once we got famous, we couldn't go because people would come in through the windows begging for a signature or a picture. I was attempting to stay up with my studies and avoid disturbances, but it became impossible and we were assigned tutors to educate us at home.

During this time, a lady named Suzanne de Passe had a significant impact on our lives. She worked for Motown and was the one who rigorously trained us after we relocated to Los Angeles. She also became the Jackson 5's manager. We occasionally lived with her, ate with her, and even played with her. We were a loud, high-spirited group, and she was young and full of life. She made a significant contribution to the formation of the Jackson 5, and I'll never be able to thank her enough for everything she did.

The Motown folks put us to the test on responses to questions we hadn't heard from anyone yet. They put us through grammatical tests. And good manners. When we were finished, they called us in for the final modifications to our sleeves and trimming of our new Afros.

After that, there was a new song to learn, "I Want You Back." The song has a narrative behind it that we gradually learned about. It was penned by Freddie Perren, a Chicago native. When we opened for Jerry Butler in a Chicago nightclub, he was Jerry Butler's pianist. He felt sad for the tiny kids recruited by the club owner, assuming the club couldn't afford to hire anyone else. When he saw us perform, his opinion changed tremendously.

"I Want You Back" was originally titled "I Want to Be Free" and was composed for Gladys Knight. Freddie even considered going over Gladys's head and giving the song to the Supremes. Instead, he told Jerry that he'd just signed this gang of Gary, Indiana students. Freddie connected the dots, understood it was us, and decided to trust fate.

Tito and Jermaine had to pay special attention when we were learning the Steeltown songs back in Gary because they were in charge of playing on those records. They listened to the guitar and bass sections on the tape for "I Want You Back," but Dad emphasised that Motown didn't expect them to play on our albums; the rhythm track would be taken care of before we put our vocals down. But he reminded them that this would increase the pressure on them to rehearse individually because we'd have to perform those songs in front of our fans. Meanwhile, we all had lyrics and prompts to memorise.

Freddy Perrin, Bobby Taylor, and Deke Richards, who, along with Hal Davis and another Motown person named "Fonce" Mizell, were part of the team that composed and produced our first songs, looked after us in the vocal area. This group was known as "The Corporation." We went over to Richards' apartment to practise, and he was impressed with how well we had prepared. He didn't have to do much tinkering with the vocal arrangement he'd worked out, and he believed we should go straight to the studio and cut our parts while we were still hot. Recording with Motown was an amazing experience for me and my brothers. Our writers moulded our music by accompanying us as we recorded it over and over again, moulding and sculpting a song until it was exactly right. We'd cut a track over and over for weeks until we got it absolutely right. And I could watch them becoming better and better as they went along. They'd tweak the phrases, the arrangements, the rhythms, everything. Berry allowed them to work in this manner because he is a perfectionist. He probably would have if they hadn't been doing it. Berry has a natural talent. He'd go into the room where we were working and tell me what I needed to do, and he'd be right. It was incredible.

"I Want You Back" sold two million copies in six weeks and reached number one when it was released in November 1969. In March 1970, we released "ABC," which sold two million albums in three weeks. I still enjoy the bit where I yell, "Siddown, girl!" I think I'm in love with you! No, get up, girl, and show me what you're capable of!" Berry's prediction came true when our third song, "The Love You Save," reached number one in June 1970.

As I previously stated, "The Corporation" at Motown produced and sculpted all of our songs in those early days. I recall numerous occasions when I felt the song should be performed one way while the producers felt it should be sung another. But I was really obedient for a long time and didn't say anything about it. It finally got to the point where I was sick of being instructed how to sing. I was fourteen years old at the time, around the period of the song "Lookin' Through the Windows." They expected me to sing in a specific style, and I knew they were mistaken. People should listen to you regardless of your age if you have it and know it. I was enraged and upset with our producers. So I called Berry Gordy and expressed my displeasure. I said that they had always told me how to sing, and I had always agreed, but suddenly they were becoming too... mechanical.

So he entered the studio and urged them to let me do anything I wanted. I believe he told them to give me greater freedom or something. And then I started adding a bunch of vocal variations that they really liked. I'd do a lot of improv, like twisting words or giving them an edge.

My three favourite songs from back then are "Never Can Say Goodbye," "I'll Be There," and "ABC." I'll never forget the first time I heard the letters "ABC." It was fantastic, in my opinion. I remember being excited to perform that song, to get into the studio and really make it work for us.

We were still rehearsing and working hard every day—some things remained the same—but we were delighted to be where we were. There were so many people rooting for us, and we were so motivated that everything seemed possible.

Everyone at Motown prepared us for success once "I Want You Back" was released. Diana loved it and had us perform in a well-known Hollywood discotheque, where she had us playing in a relaxed party environment similar to Berry's. Following Diana's event, she received an offer to perform in the "Miss Black America" telecast. Being on the show would allow us to give folks a sneak peek at our record and show. My brothers and I remembered our regret at not being able to go to New York to do our first TV show because Motown had called. We were about to start our first TV show with Motown.

We didn't work as hard on the album as we did on the single, but we had a lot of fun trying out different songs, from "Who's Lovin' You," an old Miracles song we used to do in talent shows, to "Zip-A-Dee-Doo-Dah."

We wrote songs for that album that appealed to a diverse audience—kids, teenagers, and adults—and we all agreed it was a key reason for its success. We were anxious since "The Hollywood Palace" had a live audience, a sophisticated Hollywood crowd, but we had them from the first note. Because there was an orchestra in the pit, I got to hear all of "I Want You Back" performed live for the first time because I wasn't there when they recorded the strings for the album. Like winning the citywide show in Gary, doing that show made us feel like kings.

Choosing the perfect songs for us to perform would be a significant problem now that we weren't relying on other people's hits to win over a crowd. The Corporation men and Hal Davis were assigned the task of developing and producing music specifically for us. Berry didn't want to have to bail us out once more. So, even when our initial singles reached number one, we were preoccupied with the follow-ups.

"I Want You Back" could have been performed by an adult, but "ABC" and "The Love You Save" were written specifically for our youthful voices, with sections for both Jermaine and me—another nod to the Sly sound, which rotated vocalists around the stage. The Corporation had also created those songs with dance routines in mind, both those performed by our followers at parties and those performed by us on stage. The verses were tongue-twisting, which is why Jermaine and I split them up.

Neither of those albums would have been possible without "I Want You Back." We were adding and subtracting ideas from that one mother lode of a song in the arrangements, yet the public appeared to want everything we were doing. We followed up with two more albums in the vein, "Mama's Pearl" and "Sugar Daddy," which reminded me of my own schoolyard days: "While I'm giving you the candy, he's getting all your love!" We added a fresh twist when Jermaine and I sang harmony together, which always drew applause when we did it from the same mike on stage.

According to the pros, no group started better than us. Ever.

"I'll Be There" was our true breakout song; it said, "We're here to stay." It was number one for five weeks, which is quite rare. That's a long time for a song, and it was one of my favourites out of everything we've ever done. "You and I must make a pact, we must restore salvation," I thought. Willie Hutch and Berry Gordy didn't seem like the type of individuals who would write in that manner. When we weren't in the studio, they were always making fun of us. But that music had me hooked from the first time I heard it. I had no idea what a harpsichord was until the opening notes of that record were played for us. Suzy Ikeda, my other half who stood next to me song after song, making sure I placed the correct emotion, feeling, and heart into the composition, assisted Hal Davis in producing the song. It was a sombre song, but we added a humorous interlude when I sang, "Just look over your shoulder, honey!" Without the honey, it's straight out of the legendary Four Tops song "Reach Out, I'll Be There." So we began to feel like we were a part of Motown's past as well as its future.

Originally, I was supposed to sing all of the upbeat songs while Jermaine handled the ballads. But, while Jermaine's voice was more mature at seventeen, ballads were more my love, if not really my style—yet. That was our fourth consecutive number one, and many people like Jermaine's song "I Found That Girl," the B-side of "The Love You Save," as much as the hits.

The hectic days of the major Jackson 5 tours started shortly after we gained success with our records. In the fall of 1970, we embarked on a major stadium tour, performing in venues such as Madison Square Garden and the Los Angeles Forum. When "Never Can Say Goodbye" became a great hit in 1971, we played 45 cities that summer, followed by fifty more the following year.

The majority of that time was spent in intense closeness with my brothers. We've always been a really devoted and loving group. We clowned around, had a lot of fun, and pulled ridiculous pranks on each other and the individuals that worked with us. We didn't become too rowdy—no TVs were thrown out the hotel windows—but a lot of water was dumped on various heads. We were basically attempting to get over our boredom from being on the road for so long. When you're bored on tour, you'll do anything to keep yourself entertained. We were crammed inside these hotel rooms, unable to leave due to throngs of shouting girls outside, and we wanted to have some fun. I wish we could have recorded some of what we did, especially some of the outrageous pranks. We'd all wait until Bill Bray, our security manager, fell asleep. Then we'd have absurd fast-walk races in the halls, pillow fights, tag-team wrestling matches, shaving cream wars, and whatever else we could think of. We were insane. We'd throw water balloons and paper bags off hotel balconies and watch them explode. We'd die laughing then. We flung things at each other and spent hours on the phone making phone calls and ordering massive room service meals that were brought to strangers' rooms. Anyone who entered one of our bedrooms had a 90% chance of getting wet by a pail of water pushed over the doorway.

When we arrived in a new city, we would try to see as much as we could. We travelled with a fantastic tutor, Rose Fine, who taught us a lot and made sure we did our homework. Rose instilled in me a passion for books and literature that I still have now. I devoured every book I could get my hands on. New cities provided new shopping opportunities. We enjoyed shopping, particularly in bookstores and department stores, but as our celebrity grew, our admirers turned casual shopping trips into hand-to-hand fights. Being surrounded by screaming girls was one of the most horrifying situations I'd ever had. I mean, it was difficult. We'd go into some department store to see what they had, and the fans would find out and smash the place, just tear it up. Counters would fall over, glass would shatter, and cash registers would crash. We were only interested in looking at clothes! When those mob scenes erupted, all the chaos, adoration, and recognition were too much for us to bear.

You can't imagine what it's like if you haven't seen something like that. Those ladies were dead serious. They are still. They don't realise they're hurting you since they're acting in love. They mean well, but I can attest that being mobbed hurts. You're afraid you'll suffocate or be dismembered. A thousand hands are clutching at you. One girl is tugging your wrist in this direction, while another is yanking your watch off. They grab your hair and tug it hard, and the pain is excruciating. You collide with objects, and the scrapes are excruciating. I still have the scars, and I remember where I acquired each of them. I learnt to flee past throngs of thrashing girls outside of movies, hotels, and airports early on. It's crucial to remember to hide your eyes with your hands during such emotional encounters because girls can forget they have nails. I know the fans mean well, and I appreciate their passion and support, but crowd scenes are frightening.

The first time we went to England, we witnessed the greatest mob scene I'd ever seen. We were flying over the Atlantic when the pilot revealed that he had just been advised that there were 10,000 children waiting for us at Heathrow Airport. It was impossible for us to believe. We were ecstatic, but if we could have turned around and flown home, we probably would have. We knew this was going to be interesting, but there wasn't enough fuel to return, so we flew on. When we arrived, we saw that the supporters had literally taken over the entire airport. Being mobbed like that was incredible. My brothers and I considered ourselves fortunate to have survived the airport that day.

When I was touring with the Jackson 5, I always shared a hotel room with Jermaine. He and I were close both on and offstage, and we shared many interests. Jermaine and I would get into mischief on the road since he was the sibling most enamoured by the girls who wanted to get at him.

I believe our father determined early on that he needed to keep a closer eye on us than on our other brothers. He frequently took the room next to ours, which meant he could check on us at any time via the connecting doors. I detested this arrangement, not just because he could observe our misconduct, but also because he used to abuse us. My father would bring a number of girls into the room while Jermaine and I were sleeping, fatigued from a show; when we woke up, they'd be standing there, looking at us, chuckling.

Because show business and my work were my life, the most difficult personal challenge I had to endure during my adolescence had nothing to do with recording studios or stage performances. My biggest issue back then was right there in my mirror. My identity as a human was inextricably linked to my identity as a star.

When I was approximately fourteen, my appearance began to change dramatically. My height increased significantly. People who didn't know me would walk right past me when they entered a room expecting to be introduced to cute young Michael Jackson. "I'm Michael," I'd say, and they'd seem sceptical. Michael was a cute little kid, whereas I was a gangly adolescent approaching five feet ten inches. I wasn't the person they were expecting or even wanting to see. Adolescence is difficult enough, but picture having your inherent concerns about the changes in your body exacerbated by the harsh reactions of others. They appeared startled that I could change, that my body was going through the same natural changes that everyone goes through.

It was difficult. For a long time, everyone thought I was cute, but along with all the other changes, my skin came out in a nasty case of acne. When I looked in the mirror one morning, I thought, "OH NO!" Every oil gland looked to have a pimple. And the more I thought about it, the worse it got. I didn't understand it at the time, but my oily processed food diet didn't help either.

This incident with my skin left an indelible mark on me. Because my complexion was so awful, I became really hesitant and embarrassed to meet new people. The longer I looked in the mirror, the worse the pimples seemed to get. My physical look began to depress me. So I understand how a case of acne can be terrible to a person. The effect on me was so severe that it ruined my entire personality. I couldn't look people in the eyes when I spoke to them. I'd either look down or away. I didn't feel like I had anything to be proud of, and I didn't want to go out. Nothing was done by me.

I was still pleased with our successful records, and while on stage, I didn't think about anything else. All of my concerns vanished.

But as I got offstage, I had to face that mirror again.

Things eventually changed. I began to have second thoughts about my condition. I've learned to adjust my mindset and feel better about myself. Most importantly, I altered my eating habits. That was crucial.

In the fall of 1971, I released my debut solo album, "Got to Be There." Working on the record was fantastic, and it quickly became one of my favourites. It was Berry Gordy's idea for me to do a solo recording, and as a result, I was one of the first people in a Motown group to truly break out. Berry also suggested that I record my own album. Years later, when I finally did, I found he was correct.

During that time, there was a minor quarrel that was typical of the difficulties I had as a young performer.

People often believe you're being childish and silly when you're young and have ideas. We were on tour in 1972, when "Got to Be There" was a tremendous success. "Before I sing that song, let me go offstage and grab that little hat I wore for the picture on the album cover," I told our road manager one night. The audience would go insane if they saw me wearing that hat."

It was the most absurd thing he'd ever heard, he thought. I couldn't do it because I was too young, and everyone thought it was a bad idea. Donny Osmond began wearing a very identical hat all throughout the country not long after that occurrence, and people liked it. I was confident in my intuition; I had expected it to work. When Marvin Gaye sang "Let's Get It On," he wore a hat, and everyone went crazy. When Marvin put on the hat, they knew what was going to happen. It increased the audience's involvement in the show by adding excitement and communicating something to them.

By the time "The Jackson Five" Saturday morning cartoon show debuted on network television in 1971, I was already a committed fan of film and animation. Diana Ross had increased my enjoyment of animation by teaching me to sketch, but being a cartoon character drove me over the edge into a full-fledged love of movies and the kind of animated motion pictures pioneered by Walt Disney. I admire Mr. Disney and what he accomplished with the assistance of so many outstanding artists. I am in awe of the joy he and his firm have offered to millions of children—and adults—around the world.

I had a lot of fun playing the role of a cartoon. It was great fun to get up on Saturday mornings and look forward to seeing ourselves on the screen. For all of us, it was like a dream come true.

My first major experience with movies came in 1972, when I sang the title song for the film Ben.

Ben was really important to me. Nothing has ever piqued my interest as much as going to the studio to record my voice. I had a fantastic experience. Later, when the movie came out, I'd go to the theatre and wait until the credits rolled and it said, "'Ben' sung by Michael Jackson." That really impressed me. I enjoyed both the song and the tale. Actually, the plot was similar to that of E.T. It was about a boy who became friends with a rat. People didn't comprehend the boy's attachment to this tiny creature. He was dying of some ailment, and

Ben, the leader of the rats in the city where they lived, was his sole true friend. Many others thought the film was strange, but I was not one of them. The song reached number one and remains a personal favourite of mine. I've always loved animals and enjoy reading about them and watching movies about them.

# Chapter 3: Dancing Machine

The media constantly writes bizarre things about me. I am bothered by the misrepresentation of the truth. Although I frequently hear about it, I don't usually read much of what is printed.

I'm not sure why people feel the need to make up stories about me. I suppose it's necessary to make things interesting if there's nothing scandalous to report. I take some little pride in believing that, all things considered, I did rather well. Many youngsters in the entertainment industry ended up using drugs and destroying themselves, including Frankie Lymon, Bobby Driscoll, and a number of other child stars. And, given the immense stressors placed on them at such a young age, I can understand why they would turn to narcotics. It's a tough existence. Few people are able to keep any semblance of a normal childhood.

I've never done drugs—no marijuana, no cocaine, nothing. I mean, I haven't even tried any of these things yet.

Forget about it.

That's not to say we weren't tempted. We were musicians conducting business during a time when drug usage was prevalent. I don't intend to be judgmental—it's not even a moral problem for me—but I've seen drugs destroy far too many lives to believe they're worth playing with. I'm not an angel, and I have my own terrible habits, but drugs aren't one of them.

We knew we were going across the world by the time Ben came out. Blue jeans and hamburgers had become as popular in other countries as American soul music. We were invited to join that wide world, and our first foreign tour began in 1972 with a visit to England. Even though we'd never been there or featured on British television, everyone knew every line to our songs. They even had scarves with our photographs and "Jackson 5" written in big bold letters on them. The venues were smaller than we were used to playing in the United States, but the crowds' enthusiasm was really encouraging as we finished each song. People over there could actually tell how excellent Tito was getting on the guitar since they couldn't scream during the songs as crowds back home did.

When we first visited Europe, we had three years of hits behind us, so there was enough to please both the kids who listened to our music and the Queen of England, whom we met during a Royal Command Performance. That was thrilling for us. I'd seen pictures of other bands, like the Beatles, meeting the Queen after command concerts, but I never imagined we'd get the chance to perform for her.

If Motown could have had us age anyway they wanted, they would have wanted Jackie to stay the age he was when we became a headline act and have each of us catch up with him—though I suspect they'd have preferred to keep me a year or two younger so I could still be a kid star. That may sound absurd, but it wasn't much more so than the way they were continuing to shape us, preventing us from becoming a true organisation with its own internal direction and beliefs. We were maturing and extending creatively. We had so many ideas we wanted to try, but they were adamant that we shouldn't mess with a winning recipe. At the very least, they didn't abandon us as soon as my voice changed, as some had predicted.

It got to the point where there seemed to be more males in the booth than on the studio floor at any given time. They all seemed to be knocking into each other, offering advice and listening to our music.

Our devoted fans stayed with us on songs like "I Am Love" and "Skywriter." These were musically ambitious pop recordings with intricate string arrangements, but they didn't work for us. Sure, we couldn't do "ABC" for the rest of our lives—that was the last thing we wanted—but even the older fans believed "ABC" had more going for it, which was difficult for us to accept. We were on the verge of becoming an oldies act in the mid-1970s, and I wasn't even eighteen.

Motown had come a long way from the early days when you could find skilled studio musicians supplementing their session earnings with bowling alley gigs. The music on "Dancing Machine" gained a new level of sophistication. That song contained the best horn section we'd ever worked with, as well as a "bubble machine" in the break created of synthesiser noise, which stopped the song from falling out of style completely. Disco music had its haters, but for us, it was a rite of passage into adulthood.

I loved "Dancing Machine," especially the groove and mood of the song. When it was released in 1974, I was determined to discover a dance technique that would enrich the music and make it more interesting to perform—and, hopefully, to watch.

So, when we sang "Dancing Machine" on "Soul Train," I executed the Robot, a street-style dance motion. That performance taught me about the power of television. "Dancing Machine" shot to the top of the charts overnight, and within a few days, it appeared like every youngster in America was doing the Robot. I'd never seen anything like it before.

One thing Motown and the Jackson 5 could agree on was that as our performance evolved, so should our audience. Randy had already toured with us, and Janet was demonstrating talent with her singing and dancing lessons. Randy and Janet couldn't fit into our old lineup any more than square pegs fitted into round holes. I wouldn't belittle their enormous talent by claiming that show business was so in their blood that they just took their positions as if we'd booked a seat for them. They worked hard to gain their positions in the organisation. They didn't join us since they shared our old toys and ate meals with us.

If you only went by blood, I'd be equal parts crane operator and vocalist. These things are impossible to quantify. Dad worked us hard and had specific goals in mind while we were sleeping.

We had previously performed sketches in a 1971 TV special called Goin' Back to Indiana, which commemorated our first visit to Gary. Since our last visit to our hometown, our records have become worldwide hits.

It was even more fun to perform skits with nine of us instead of just five, plus any guests who decided to show up. Dad was overjoyed with our extended lineup. In retrospect, I know the Las Vegas gigs were an experience I'll never forget. We didn't have a high-pressure concert audience that demanded only our hit tunes. We were temporarily relieved of the need to keep up with what everyone else was doing. Every show included a ballad or two to help break in my "new voice." I had to think about things like that when I was fifteen.

There were clues that other Motown organisations were changing by the time we started putting our own act together. Marvin Gaye took command of his own songs and produced What's Going On, his finest record. Stevie Wonder was learning more about electronic keyboards than the studio's seasoned hired guns, and they were turning to him for help. One of our favourite Motown memories is Stevie leading us in shouting to support his difficult, controversial song "You Haven't Done Nothin'." Though Stevie and Marvin remained in the Motown camp, they had fought for – and won – the ability to make their own albums, as well as publish their own tunes. Motown hadn't even moved an inch with us. We were still children to them, even if they weren't clothed or "protecting" us.

Our issues with Motown began in 1974, when we told them unequivocally that we wanted to develop and produce our own songs. Simply put, we didn't like how our music sounded at the moment. We had a strong competitive impulse and were threatened by other groups that were crafting a more current sound.

When I sense that something is amiss, I must speak up. Most people don't think of me as tough or self-assured, but that's because they don't know me. My brothers and I eventually reached a point with Motown when we were unhappy but no one said anything. My brothers remained silent. My father remained silent. It was up to me to set up a meeting with Berry Gordy and speak with him. I was the one who had to announce that we, the Jackson 5, were leaving Motown. I went up to confront him, and it was one of the most difficult things I'd ever done. I might have kept my mouth shut if I had been the only one of us who was upset, but there had been so much talk at home about how miserable we were all that I went in and talked to him and told him how we felt. I told him I was dissatisfied.

Remember that I adore Berry Gordy. I believe he is a genius, a clever man who is one of the music industry's titans. I have nothing but admiration for him, but on that particular day, I was a lion. I grumbled that we weren't given the flexibility to develop and produce music. He said he still believed we required outside producers to make hit records.

But I was aware of the situation. Berry was yelling in rage. That was a difficult encounter, but we're friends again, and he's still like a father to me—proud of me and delighted in my accomplishment. Berry will always be special to me since he taught me some of the most important lessons I've ever learned. He's the one who informed the Jackson 5 that they'd go down in history, and that's exactly what occurred. Over the years, Motown has done so much for so many individuals. I consider ourselves fortunate to have been one of the groups Berry directly presented to the world, and I owe him a great debt of gratitude. Without him, my life would have been drastically different. We all believed that Motown launched our professional careers. We all felt like we had roots there and wanted us to stay. We appreciated everything they had done for us, but change is unavoidable. I'm a person of the moment, and I have to inquire, "How are things now?" What is going on now? What will happen in the future that will have an impact on what has happened in the past?

I sensed it was time for a change, so we went with our gut impulses and won when we chose to go for a new start with another label, Epic.

We were relieved that we had finally expressed our feelings and severed the bonds that held us together, but we were also devastated when Jermaine opted to stay with Motown. His situation was more problematic than ours because he was Berry's son-in-law. He believed that staying was more important than leaving, and Jermaine always followed his conscience, so he left the organisation.

Because it was so traumatic for me, I vividly recall the first show we did without him. Jermaine had been standing to my left with his bass since my first days on stage, and even in our rehearsals in our Gray living room. I relied on being around Jermaine. And the first time I performed without him, with no one next to me, I felt completely naked onstage for the first time in my life. So we pushed even harder to make up for the loss of one of our brightest stars, Jermaine. I recall that event vividly because we received three standing ovations. We put in a lot of effort.

When Jermaine departed the group, Marlon stepped in, and he truly flourished onstage. Randy, my younger brother, officially took over as bongo player and band baby.

Things became even more problematic for us around the time Jermaine left since we were filming a terrible summer replacement TV series. I made a bad decision by agreeing to do the show, and I despised every minute of it.

I used to enjoy watching the old "Jackson Five" cartoon show. On

Saturday mornings, I'd wake up and exclaim, "I'm a cartoon!" But I despised performing this television show because I believed it would harm rather than enhance our recording career. A TV series, in my opinion, is the worst thing a music artist can do. "But this is going to hurt our record sales," I kept repeating. Others responded, "No, it's going to help them."

They were completely incorrect. We had to dress ridiculously and execute absurd comic routines to canned laughter. It was all so phoney. We didn't have enough time to learn or master television. To achieve a deadline, we had to compose three dance numbers per day. Week after week, the Nielsen ratings ruled our lives. It's something I'd never do again. It's a dead end street. What occurs is partially psychological. You visit people's houses every week, and they get the impression that they know you too well. You're doing all this ridiculous comedy to canned laughs, and your music fades into the background. You can't get serious again and resume your profession where you left off because you're overexposed. People think of you as the ones that do the ridiculous, wild routines. You're Santa Claus one week, Prince Charming the next, and a rabbit the next. It's insane because you lose your individuality in the company; your rocker image vanishes. I'm not a stand-up comic. I'm not a television host. I work as a musician. That is why I declined opportunities to host the Grammys and the American Music Awards. Is it really entertaining for me to walk up there and make people laugh because I'm Michael Jackson, even if I know deep down that I'm not funny?

I remember playing theatres-in-the-round after our TV program when the stage didn't spin because if they had, we would have been singing to some empty seats. That experience taught me something, and I was the one who declined to renew our deal with the network for another season. I simply told my father and brothers that I believed it was a huge mistake, and they agreed with me. I had some reservations about the show before we began filming, but I eventually agreed to give it a shot because everyone thought it would be a terrific experience for us.

The difficulty with television is that everything has to be jammed into a small amount of time. There isn't time to perfect anything. Your life is ruled by routines—tight schedules. If you're not satisfied with something, you simply forget about it and move on to the next routine. By nature, I am a perfectionist. I like things to be as good as they can be. I want people to hear or see what I've done and know that I gave it my all. That is something I feel I owe an audience. Our sets for the program were untidy, the lighting was frequently poor, and our choreography was rushed. The concert was a huge success in certain ways. We beat out a popular show on the opposing channel in the Nielsen ratings. CBS was desperate to keep us, but I felt that show was a disaster. As it turned out, it harmed our record sales, and it took us a while to recover. When you know something isn't right for you, you must make difficult choices and trust your instincts.

We had cut some demos of our songs at home during our breaks from shooting, but we chose to hold off releasing those since we didn't want to put a gun to anyone's head. We knew Philly had a lot to offer us, so we decided to keep our surprise for later.

Our two songs, "Blues Away" and "Style of Life," were difficult to keep a secret because we were so proud of them at the time. "Style of Life" was a Tito-directed jam that kept us in the nightclub beat that "Dancing Machine" had gotten us into, but we kept it a little leaner and meaner than Motown would have cut it.

"Blues Away" was one of my earliest songs, and while I no longer sing it, I'm not ashamed to hear it. I couldn't have continued in this field if I had come to despise my own work after all that effort. It's a bright song about overcoming deep depression—I tried to channel Jackie Wilson's "Lonely Teardrops" style of laughing on the outside to halt the churning inside.

We were astonished to realise that we all looked the same when we saw the cover art for The Jacksons' record, the first we cut for Epic. Tito, too, appeared to be underweight! I had my "crown" Afro at the time, so I didn't stand out as much. Even yet, when we played new songs like "Enjoy Yourself" and "Show You the Way to Go," people realised I was still second from the left, right in front. Randy grabbed Tito's old spot on my far right, while Tito moved into Jermaine's old spot. As I already stated, it took a long time for me to be comfortable with that, despite Tito's error.

Those two tracks were enjoyable to listen to—"Enjoy Yourself" was wonderful for dancing. It has some really great horns and rhythm guitar. It was also a number-one hit. For my tastes, I preferred "Show You the Way to Go" because it demonstrated the Epic team's high esteem for our singing. We were all over that record, and it was our best. I adored the high hat and the strings flowing alongside us like bird wings. I'm shocked that the song wasn't a bigger success.

Going Places, our second Epic album, was unlike our first. There were fewer dance tunes and more songs with messages. We understood the idea of promoting peace and letting music take over was a wonderful one, but it reminded us of the old O'Jays' "Love Train" and was not really our style.

Still, the lack of a big pop hit on "Going Places" may have been a good thing because it made "Different Kind of Lady" an easy candidate for club play. It was in the middle of side one, sandwiched between two Gamble & Huff tracks, and our song stood out like a ball of fire. That was a real band cooking, with the Philly horns adding exclamation points after exclamation points, just as we'd imagined. That's the vibe we were looking for when we were demoing with our old pal Bobby Taylor before signing with Epic. Kenny and Leon added the finishing touches, the icing, but we prepared the cake ourselves.

Even as we were leaving the firm, Motown had purchased the rights to film the Broadway musical The Wiz. The Wiz was an updated, darker version of the classic film The Wizard of Oz, which I had long admired. When I was a kid, The Wizard of Oz was only shown on television once a year, on a Sunday night. Because they've grown up with videocassettes and the additional watching options that cable gives, today's kids can't comprehend what a big deal that was for all of us.

I'd also seen the Broadway production, which was fantastic. I swear I saw it 6 or 7 times. I eventually became friends with the show's star, Stephanie Mills, who played Broadway Dorothy. I told her at the time, and I've always thought it was a tragedy that her performance in the play couldn't be captured on video. I sobbed over and over. As much as I admire the Broadway stage, I doubt I'd want to perform on it. When you deliver a performance, whether live or recorded, you want to be able to judge it, to measure yourself, and to try to improve. You can't do it in an unrecorded or untape performance. It makes me sad to think of all the wonderful actors who have played roles we would give anything to see but are no longer available to us because they couldn't or didn't want to be recorded.

If I had been persuaded to go onstage, it would have been to work with Stephanie, despite the fact that her performances were so compelling that I might have sobbed in front of the audience. Motown purchased The Wiz for one reason, and in my opinion, it was the finest reason possible: Diana Ross.

I auditioned for the position of the Scarecrow because I thought his character suited my personality the best. I was too bouncy for the Tin Man and too light for the Lion, so I had a specific objective in mind, and I worked hard on my reading and dancing for the part. When I got the call back from the director, Sidney Lumet, I was both proud and terrified. Making a film was a new experience for me, and I would have to let go of my commitments to my family and music for months. I'd been to New York, where we were filming, to get a sense of Harlem for The Wiz's tale, but I'd never lived there. I was shocked at how fast I adjusted to the new way of life. I had a great time meeting individuals I'd always heard about on the opposite coast but had never met.

I was searching, both consciously and unconsciously, during this time in my life. I was stressed and worried about what I wanted to accomplish with my life now that I was an adult. I was weighing my alternatives and preparing to make decisions that could have far-reaching consequences. It was like being in a gigantic school on the set of The Wiz. My skin was still a disaster during the filming, so I found myself actually loving the makeup. It was a fantastic makeup job. Mine took five hours to complete, and we didn't shoot on Sundays. We finally got it down to four hours after doing it for so long. The other folks who were being acted out were astounded that I didn't mind sitting there for such lengthy lengths of time. They despised it, but I enjoyed having it applied to my face. It was the most amazing thing in the world when I was converted into the Scarecrow. I was able to flee by pretending to be someone else. Kids would come to the set and I'd have a great time playing with them and responding to them as the Scarecrow.

I'd always imagined myself doing something really elegant in the movies, but my time in New York with the makeup, costume, and prop experts opened my eyes to another part of how wonderful filmmaking could be. I had always admired Charlie Chaplin's films, and no one ever saw him doing anything obviously elegant during his silent film days. In my Scarecrow, I wanted something of the calibre of his characters. Everything about the costume was fantastic, from the coil legs to the tomato nose to the fright wig. I even preserved the orange and white sweater that came with it and wore it to a photo shoot years later.

The film included fantastic, intricate dance pieces that were easy to learn. However, this created an unexpected issue with my co-stars.

I've been able to observe someone execute a dance step and immediately know how to do it since I was a small child. Another person may need to be guided through the activity step by step, telling them to count and to place this leg here and the hip to the right. Put your neck over there when your hip moves to the left... that sort of thing. But if I envision it, I can make it happen.

When we were filming The Wiz, I was being taught the choreography alongside my co-stars—the Tin Man, the Lion, and Diana Ross—and they were becoming irritated. I had no idea what was wrong until Diana pulled me away and told me that I was humiliating her. I just stood there staring at her. Putting Diana Ross down? Me? She stated she knew I wasn't aware of it, but I was picking up the dances at an alarming rate. It was humiliating for her and the others, who couldn't learn the steps after seeing the choreographer do them. He'd show us something, she said, and I'd just walk out there and do it. It took them longer to learn when he asked the others to do it. We laughed about it, but I tried to disguise the ease with which I mastered my steps.

I also discovered that there is a slightly nefarious side to the filmmaking business. When I stood in front of the camera, trying to do a serious scene, one of the other actors would start making funny expressions at me. I had always been taught real professionalism and preparedness, so I thought that was a very cruel thing to do. This actor would be aware that I had critical lines to say that day, but he would make these ridiculous faces to divert my attention. It was more than thoughtless and unfair to me.

Marlon Brando later told me that people used to do that to him all the time.

The set problems were few and few between, and it was amazing to work so closely with Diana. She's a stunningly gorgeous and talented woman. Making this film with you was a very unique experience for me. I adore her to pieces. I've always had a soft spot for her.

Even though I was having fun, the entire Wiz period was a source of tension and concern for me. I remember July 4th of that year vividly because I was at my brother Jermaine's house, which was about a half-block away along the shore. I was playing in the waves when I realised I couldn't breathe. No air. Nothing. What was the problem, I wondered? I tried not to panic, but I dashed back home to fetch Jermaine, who drove me to the hospital. It was a wild ride. A blood artery in my lung had burst. It never happened again, though I used to get small pinches and jerks in there that were probably just my imagination. This disorder was eventually discovered to be related to pleurisy. My doctor urged that I attempt to take things slowly, but my schedule would not allow that. Hard effort remained the name of the game.

My character has a lot to say and a lot to learn. I was propped up on my pole, surrounded by crows who were laughing at me while I sang "You Can't Win." The song was about embarrassment and powerlessness, which many people have experienced at some point in their lives, and the feeling that there are individuals out there who don't aggressively hold you back as much as they work silently on your fears so that you hold yourself back. The writing was smart, showing me plucking bits of knowledge and quotations out of my straw while having no idea what to do with them. My straw had all the answers, but I didn't know what the questions were.

While I was pondering what I should do next, another man and I were on parallel tracks that would eventually lead us to the set of The Wiz. We were rehearsing in Brooklyn one day, and we were reading our parts out to one another. I expected line learning to be the most difficult thing I'd ever accomplish, but I was pleasantly pleased. Everyone had been helpful, assuring me that it would be simpler than

I imagined. That it was.

That day, we were filming the crows scene. Because they'd be dressed as crows, the other males wouldn't even have their heads visible in this scene. They seemed to know their parts inside and out. I'd studied mine as well, but I'd only pronounced them out once or twice.

The instructions instructed me to take a piece of paper from my straw and read it. It was a quotation. At the end, the author's name, Socrates, was printed. I'd read Socrates, but I'd never heard his name pronounced, so I said, "Soh-crates," because that's how I'd always believed it was. There was a little pause before I heard someone say, "Soc-ruh-teeze." I turned to face this man I barely recognized. He wasn't one of the actors, but he seemed to fit in. I remember thinking he had a nice smile and seemed extremely self-assured.

I smiled, a little ashamed about mispronouncing the name, and thanked him for his assistance. His face was eerily familiar, and I was certain I had met him previously. By extending his hand, he reinforced my fears.

"It's Quincy Jones. "I'm keeping the score."

# Chapter 4: Me And Q

I first met Quincy Jones when I was approximately twelve years old in Los Angeles. Quincy later told me that Sammy Davis, Jr. had told him at the time that "this kid is gonna be the next biggest thing since sliced bread." Something along those lines, at any rate, and Quincy said, "Oh yeah?" I was little at the time, but I recall Sammy Davis introducing me to Q.

Our connection blossomed on the set of The Wiz and evolved into a father-and-son relationship. "Look, I'm going to do an album—do you think you could recommend some producers?" I called him after The Wiz.

I wasn't teasing. My question was simple yet sincere. We spoke about music for a while, and after a few names and some hedging and hawing, he replied, "Why don't you let me do it?"

I honestly hadn't considered it. He thought I was teasing him, but I wasn't. I simply didn't think he'd be interested in my music. So I stuttered something along the lines of, "Oh sure, great idea." I never considered it."

Quincy still makes fun of me about it.

Anyway, we started planning the record that became Off the Wall right away.

My brothers and I decided to start our own production firm and began brainstorming titles.

There aren't many articles on peacocks in the papers, but about this time, I came across the only one that mattered. I had always adored peacocks and had admired one that Berry Gordy had at one of his residences. So I was ecstatic when I read the article, which included a photo of a peacock and disclosed a lot about the bird's traits. I believed I had discovered the photograph we were looking for. It was a detailed work, a touch dry in spots, but interesting. According to the author, the peacock's complete plumage would only explode when it was in love, at which point all the hues would shine—all the colours of the rainbow on one body.

That lovely photograph and its meaning immediately captivated me. The plumage of that bird provided the message I was seeking to explain the Jacksons and our great attachment to one another, as well as our diverse hobbies. My brothers liked the concept, so we named our new company Peacock Productions to avoid leaning too much on the Jackson name. Our first world tour was on bringing people of all ethnicities together via music. Some people we knew were perplexed when we talked of bringing all races together via music—after all, we were black musicians. "Music is colorblind," we said. Every night, especially in Europe and other parts of the world we had travelled, we witnessed this. The people we met there were enthusiastic about our music. It didn't matter to them what colour our skin was or where we lived.

We wanted to establish ourselves as a fresh presence in the music world, not just as singers and dancers, but also as authors, composers, arrangers, producers, and even publishers, so we decided to develop our own production company. We had so many interests that we required an umbrella firm to keep track of them all. CBS had agreed to let us make our own album—the previous two albums had sold well, but "Different Kind of Lady" had a possibility worth developing. They did have one condition for us: they assigned an A&R man, Bobby Colomby, who used to be with Blood, Sweat, and Tears, to check in with us on a regular basis to see how we were doing and if we needed any assistance. We understood that the five of us required some other musicians to achieve the finest sound possible, and we were lacking in two areas: keyboard and arranging. We had been carefully incorporating all of the latest technology into our Encino studio without truly mastering it. Greg Phillinganes was young for a studio pro, but that was a plus in our eyes since we wanted someone who would be more open to fresh ways of doing things than the seasoned veterans we'd worked with over the years.

He came to Encino for pre production work, and we all surprised each other. Our mutual preconceptions have just vanished. It was fascinating to see. We told him that we enjoyed the vocal tracks that Philly International always put a premium on, but when the mix came out, we always seemed to be fighting someone else's wall of sound, all those strings and percussion. We wanted a cleaner, more funky sound, with a flintier bass and sharper trumpet lines. Greg put into musical form what we were sketching for him and then some with his lovely rhythm arrangements. He seemed to be reading our minds.

Paulinho de Costa, a Bobby Colomby recruit who came to work with us at the time, was someone we were concerned about because Randy seemed to be told he couldn't do all the percussion on his own. However, Paulinho took the Brazilian samba tradition of adapting and playing on rudimentary, often homemade instruments with him. We seemed to have the entire planet covered when de Costa's sound combined with Randy's more traditional approach.

We were stuck between a rock and a hard place in terms of creativity. We'd worked with the world's sharpest, hippest pop guys at Motown and Philly International, and we'd be fools to dismiss what we'd learned from them, but we couldn't be imitated. Fortunately, Bobby Colomby introduced us to a song called "Blame It on the Boogie." It was a fast-paced, finger-poppin' song that was a terrific vehicle for the band approach we were trying to build. I had a good time slurring the chorus: "Blame It on the Boogie" could be uttered in one breath without my lips touching. We had some fun with the credits on the record's inside cover; "Blame It on the Boogie" was composed by three guys from England, one of them was named Michael Jackson. It was an astonishing coincidence. Writing disco songs came naturally to me because I was used to having dance breaks inserted into all of the major songs I was asked to perform.

There was a lot of excitement and anxiety about our future. We were going through a lot of artistic and personal transformations, including changes in our music, family relationships, and dreams and goals. All of this made me reconsider how I was spending my time, especially in comparison to other individuals my age. I had always carried a lot of responsibility, but now it seemed like everyone wanted a piece of me. There wasn't much to go around, and I had to be accountable to myself. I had to take stock of my life and decide who I was going to devote my all to and what people desired from me. It was difficult for me, but I had to learn to be cautious of some of the individuals around me. God was at the top of my priority list, followed by my mother, father, and siblings and sisters. I was reminded of Clarence Carter's classic song "Patches," in which the oldest son is asked to take care of the farm when his father dies, and his mother tells him she depends on him. We weren't sharecroppers, and I wasn't the eldest, but those were slender shoulders to bear such weights. For some reason, I've always found it tough to say no to my family and other individuals I care about. I would agree to do something or take care of something even if I was concerned that it would be too much for me.

I was frequently emotional and under a lot of stress. You can't keep your emotions bottled up for long when you're stressed. Many people wondered how serious I was about music after hearing about my newfound interest in movies after appearing in one. It was implied that my decision to audition had occurred at an inconvenient time for the new band's formation. To outsiders, it appeared to arrive just as we were ready to get started. But, of course, everything turned out well.

"That's What You Get for Being Polite" was my way of admitting that I wasn't living in an ivory tower and that I, like all older teenagers, had insecurities and uncertainties. I was concerned that the world and all it had to offer would pass me by as I worked to become the best in my area.

On the first Epic album, there was a Gamble and Huff song called "Dreamer" that had this subject, and as I was learning it, I felt they could have written it with me in mind. I've always been a romantic. I set objectives for myself. I look at things and try to imagine what is conceivable, hoping to go over those limits.

I became twenty-one in 1979 and began to take full charge of my career. My father's personal management contract with me expired around this time, and despite the fact that it was a difficult decision, the contract was not extended.

It's not simple to fire your father.

But I didn't appreciate how some issues were being handled. Combining family and business can be difficult. It might be fantastic or terrible depending on the relationship. Even under the best of circumstances, it is a difficult task.

Did it affect my connection with my father? I'm not sure if it did in his heart, but it didn't in mine. It was a decision I knew I had to make since I was starting to feel like I was working for him rather than him working for me. And we are two very different people when it comes to creativity. He would propose things that I would strongly oppose because they were inappropriate for me. All I wanted was to be in charge of my own life. And I accepted it. I had no choice. Everyone, sooner or later, reaches that stage, and I had been in the business for a long time. I was quite experienced for a twenty-one-year-old—a fifteen-year veteran. We were anxious to take the Destiny band and concept on the road, but I became hoarse from doing so many performances and singing so much. No one held it against me when we had to cancel several shows, but I felt like I was holding my brothers back after the excellent job they had done when we worked together to get us all back on track. We made some improvised changes to relieve the strain on my throat. Marlon took over for me in some passages where I needed to hold extended notes. Our set piece on the album, "Shake Your Body (Down to the Ground)," proved to be a lifesaver for us onstage because we already had a fantastic jam in the studio to expand on. It was disappointing to have finally accomplished our aim of having our own music as the showpiece rather than a novelty tune, only to be unable to give it our all. But it wasn't long before it was our turn.

In retrospect, I think I was more patient than my brothers expected. While we were remixing Destiny, it came to me that we had "left out" some topics that I hadn't discussed with my brothers since I wasn't sure they'd be as intrigued as I was. Epic had agreed in the deal to handle any solo albums I might choose to do. Perhaps they were hedging their bets; if the Jacksons' new sound didn't succeed, they could try to form me into something they could mould for the rest of my life. That may appear to be a questionable way of thinking, but I knew from experience that money people are constantly interested in what is going on, what can happen, and how to repay their investment. It made sense for them to think that way. In light of what has happened subsequently, I question those views I had, but they were genuine at the time.

Destiny was our most successful album, and we knew we'd arrived when people bought your record because they knew you were good and would give them your all on every song and every album. My first solo record has to be the greatest it could be.

I didn't want Off the Wall to sound like Destiny outtakes. That's why I wanted to bring in an outside producer who wouldn't come in with preconceived preconceptions about how the production should sound. I also needed someone with a decent ear to assist me in selecting content because I didn't have enough time to write two sides of songs that I was proud of. I was aware that the public anticipated more than two good songs on an album, particularly in discos with their lengthy cuts, and I wanted the fans to be satisfied.

All of these factors contributed to Quincy being the best producer I could have wished for. Quincy Jones's pals referred to him as "Q" for short because of his love of BBQ. Later, after we'd finished Off the Wall, he invited me to a concert of his symphonic music at the Hollywood Bowl, but I was so bashful at the time that I stood in the wings, just like I had as a youngster, to watch the show. He stated he expected more from me, and we've been trying to meet each other's expectations ever since.

When I phoned him to ask his opinion on a producer, he began talking about people in the industry—who I could work with and who I'd have problems with. He knew who was booked, who would be too relaxed, and who would put the "pedal to the metal." He was more familiar with Los Angeles than Mayor Bradley, and that was how he kept up with what was going on. As a jazz arranger, orchestrator, and film composer, he was a helpful guide for those on the outside looking in when it came to pop music. I was relieved that my outside source was a good buddy who also proved to be the ideal producer pick. He had access to a wealth of talent through his contacts, and he was an excellent listener as well as a clever man.

Girlfriend was the working title for the Off the Wall album. Before they ever met me, Paul and Linda McCartney penned a song with that title in mind.

Paul McCartney always tells people about the time I called him and suggested we compose some hit tunes together.

But it wasn't how we originally met.

I first encountered Paul at a party on the Queen Mary, which is docked in Long Beach. Heather, his daughter, acquired my phone number from someone and called to invite me to this enormous party. She enjoyed our music, so we started conversing. Paul and his family were in Los Angeles as his Wings over America tour concluded. They invited me to the Harold Lloyd estate for a party. At that party, Paul McCartney and I first met. We shook hands in the midst of a large crowd, and he remarked, "You know, I've written a song for you." I was taken aback and thanked him. At the party, he began singing "Girlfriend" to me.

So we swapped phone numbers and made plans to get up soon, but different projects and life just got in the way for both of us, and we didn't talk for a couple of years. He eventually included the song on his own CD, London Town.

When we were working on Off the Wall, Quincy approached me one day and said, "Michael, I've got a song that's perfect for you." He played "Girlfriend" for me, not realising that Paul had composed it specifically for me. He was surprised and thrilled when I told him. We recorded it shortly after and included it on the CD. It was a fantastic coincidence.

Quincy and I discussed Off the Wall and meticulously plotted the sound we wanted. When he asked what I most wanted to happen in the studio, I told him we had to sound different than the Jacksons. It was difficult to utter those words, given how hard we'd worked to become the Jacksons, but Quincy understood what I meant, and together we made an album that reflected our goal. "Rock with You," the smash hit track, was exactly what I was going for. It was ideal for me to sing and dance to. Rod Temperton, whom Quincy knew from his work with the band Heatwave on "Boogie Nights," had written the song with a more aggressive, get-down arrangement in mind, but Quincy softened the onslaught and slid in a synthesiser that sounded like the insides of a conch shell on a beach. Q and I both admired

Rod's work and finally requested him to work on stylizing three of his tracks, including the title cut, for me. Rod and I shared many similarities. He, like myself, felt more at ease singing and writing about the nightlife than going out and experiencing it. It always amazes me when people believe that something created by an artist is based on a true experience or reflects his or her own lifestyle. Nothing could be further from the truth in many cases. I know I sometimes draw on my own experiences, but I sometimes hear and read things that spark an idea for a song. The imagination is an artist's most powerful instrument. It can generate a desired mood or experience, as well as transport you to another location entirely.

Quincy gave the arrangers and musicians a lot of leeway in the studio, maybe with the exception of symphonic arrangements, which are his specialty. While the studio personnel were lining up for the date, I took Greg Phillinganes, a member of the Destiny crew, over to "run the floor" on numbers that he and I had worked on together in Encino. Greg was joined on percussion by Paulinho da Costa, and Randy made a cameo appearance on "Don't Stop Til You Get Enough."

Quincy is incredible and does not simply choose yes-men to do his bidding. I've spent my entire life with professionals, and I can tell who is trying to stay up, who can produce, and who can cross swords constructively once in a while without losing sight of the shared aim. We had Louis "Thunder Thumbs" Johnson, who had worked on the Brothers Johnson recordings with Quincy. Wah Wah Watson, Mario Henderson, David Williams, and Larry Carlton from the Crusaders also played guitar on the record. George Duke, Phil Upchurch, and Richard Heath were chosen from the crème of the jazz/funk crop, yet they never hinted that this music was anything but what they were used to. Quincy and I had an excellent working relationship, so we shared responsibilities and often checked in with one another.

Quincy hadn't done much dance music before Off the Wall, so on

"Don't Stop Til You Get Enough," "Working Day and Night," and "Get on the Floor," Greg and I collaborated to create a thicker wall of sound at Quincy's studio. "Get on the Floor," though not a single, was particularly fulfilling because Louis Johnson gave me a smooth-enough bottom to ride in the verses and then let me come back stronger with each chorus. Quincy's engineer, Bruce Swedien, put the finishing touches on that mix, which I still enjoy hearing.

"Working Day and Night" was Paulinho's showpiece, and my background vocals raced to keep up with his grab bag of toys. To eliminate any remaining echo, Greg built up a prepared electric piano with the tone of a perfect acoustic piano. The lyrical topic was similar to "The Things I Do for You" from Destiny, but because this was a refinement of something I'd said previously, I wanted to keep it simple and let the music carry the song.

The whispered intro to "Don't Stop Til You Get Enough" was used to build suspense and surprise listeners with the swirling strings and percussion. It was also unique due to my voice arrangement. On the track, I sing in overdubs as a group. To fit in with the music I was hearing in my brain, I composed a high part that my solo voice couldn't handle on its own, so I let the arrangement take over from the singing. Q's fade out was incredible, with guitars chopping like kalimbas, or African thumb pianos. That song has special meaning for me because it was the first song I created as a whole. "Don't Stop Til You Get Enough" was my first big break, and it immediately soared to number one. It was the tune that earned me my first Grammy nomination. Quincy had faith in me enough to urge me to go into the studio on my own, which I appreciated. Then he added strings, which was the cherry on top.

Off the Wall became a Michael Jackson album because of the ballads. I'd done ballads with the brothers before, but they weren't very fond of them and did them more as a favour to me than anything else. In addition to "Girlfriend," Off the Wall had a slick, engaging tune called "I Can't Help It" that was memorable and great pleasure to sing but a little quirkier than a nice song like "Rock with You."

Two of the biggest hits were "Off the Wall" and "Rock with You." So much up-tempo dance music is threatening, but I appreciated the gentle coaxing, taking a shy girl and letting her shred her anxieties rather than forcing them out of her. I returned to a high-pitched voice on Off the Wall, but "Rock with You" demanded a more natural tone. If you were throwing a party, I thought those two songs would attract people in the door, and the tougher boogie music would send everyone home happy. There was also "She's Out of My Life." Perhaps it was too personal for a party.

It was intended for me. Even when I know my dates well, it might be difficult for me to look them in the eyes. My dating and romantic interactions with women have not resulted in the joyful ending I desired. Something constantly gets in the way. What I share with millions of people is not the same as what you share with one. Many girls want to know what makes me tick—why I live the way I do or why I do the things I do—in an attempt to get inside my head. They want to save me from loneliness, but they do it in such a way that I get the idea they want to share my loneliness, which I wouldn't wish on anyone, because I believe I'm one of the world's loneliest individuals.

"She's Out of My Life" is about realising that the boundaries that have separated me from others are temptingly low and look to be easy to jump over, yet they remain in place while what I truly love fades from view. Tom Bahler composed a lovely bridge that seemed straight out of a Broadway musical. In reality, such challenges are not easily remedied, and the song depicts this truth by implying that the problem cannot be conquered. We couldn't place this song at the opening or end of the album since it would have been too depressing. That's why, when Stevie's song comes on later, so slowly and carefully, like if unlocking a bolted-closed door, I still say, "Whew."

The spell is broken by the time Rod's "Burn This Disco Out" finishes the LP.

But I was too preoccupied with "She's Out of My Life." In one case, the narrative is true—I cried at the end of a take because the lyrics had such an immediate impact on me. I had let so much accumulate within me. I was twenty-one years old, and I was rich in some experiences and lacking in genuine joy. Sometimes I envision my existence as an image in one of those circus trick mirrors, thick in one section and thin to the point of disappearance in another. I was scared that it might appear on "She's Out of My Life," but if it touched people's hearts, I'd feel less lonely.

Q and Bruce Swedien were the only individuals who were with me when I became emotional after that take. I recall burying my face in my hands and hearing nothing but the hum of the equipment as my tears resonated around the room. I apologised later, but they claimed there was no need.

Despite its eventual success, making Off the Wall was one of the most trying moments of my life. At the time, I had few close friends and felt very isolated. I was so lonely that I used to stroll around my neighbourhood expecting to meet someone with whom I could converse and possibly make friends. I wanted to meet people who were unfamiliar with who I was. I hoped to meet someone who would be my buddy because they liked me and needed a friend as well, not because of who I am. I wanted to meet everyone in the neighbourhood, including the youngsters.

Loneliness is unavoidable with success. That is correct. People assume you're fortunate and have everything. They believe you can go anywhere and do anything, but that isn't the case. One yearns for the fundamentals.

I've learned to deal with these things better now, and I'm not nearly as depressed as I used to be. When I was in school, I didn't have many girlfriends. There were some girls I thought were cute, but I couldn't bring myself to approach them. I was too embarrassed—I'm not sure why—it was insane. One girl in particular was a good buddy of mine. I liked her, but I was too shy to tell her so.

Tatum O'Neal was my first genuine date. We met at On the Rox, a Sunset Strip club. We swapped phone numbers and communicated frequently. I talked to her for hours, on the road, in the studio, and at home. We went to a party at Hugh Hefner's Playboy Mansion on our first date and had a terrific time. That night at On the Rox, she had grasped my hand for the first time. I was sitting at this table when we met, and I felt this smooth hand reach over and grab mine. Tatum was the one. This probably doesn't mean much to most people, but it meant a lot to me. She made contact with me. That was my impression. Girls had always touched me on tour in the past, grabbing at me and shouting behind a wall of security guards. But this was different; it was one-on-one, which is usually great.

Ours grew into a really tight friendship. We were quite close for a long time after I fell in love with her (and she with me). The relationship eventually evolved into a strong friendship. We still chat from time to time, and I guess you could say she was my first love—after Diana.

I was pleased for Diana Ross when I heard she was getting married because I knew it would bring her great joy. Still, it was difficult for me because I had to walk around seeming to be shocked that Diana was marrying this man I'd never met. I wanted her to be happy, but I have to admit that I was a little upset and jealous because I've always loved Diana and will continue to do so.

Brooke Shields was another crush. For a while, we were romantically serious. There have been many great ladies in my life, whose names would be meaningless to the readers of this book, and it would be unfair to mention them because they are not celebrities and are not used to having their names printed. I appreciate my privacy, therefore I respect theirs as well.

Liza Minelli is someone whose friendship I will always treasure. She's similar to my showbiz sister. We get together and chat about business; it seeps through our pores. We both eat, sleep, and drink different moves, tunes, and dance. We have so much fun together. I adore her.

I started working on the Triumph album with my brothers immediately after we finished Off the Wall. For our tour, we wanted to incorporate the best of both albums. "Can You Feel It?" was the album's first single, and it was the Jacksons' closest approach to a rock feel. It wasn't really dancing music. We had it in mind for the opening video of our tour, similar to our own Also Sprach Zarathustra, the 2001 theme. Jackie and I had discussed blending the band sound with a gospel/children's choir vibe. In a way, it was an homage to Gamble and Huff, because the song was about love triumphing and healing the world's sins. Randy's singing is fantastic, even if his range isn't as wide as he'd like it to be. When we sang it, his breathing and phrasing had me on my toes. I worked for hours on a brilliant foghorn-style keyboard, going over it and over it again until I got it just right. We had six minutes, which I don't believe was too lengthy.

"Lovely One" was an expansion of "Shake Your Body Down to the Ground," injected with a lighter Off the Wall vibe. On Jackie's "Your Ways," I tried out a newer, more ethereal voice, with the keyboards giving a distant air. Paulinho took out all the heavy weapons: triangles, skulls, and gongs. This song is about a quirky girl who is who she is, and there's nothing I can do about it but enjoy it while I can.

Mike McKinney propels "Everybody" like a jet turning and bearing down, making it more fun than the Off the Wall dance numbers. The background vocals hint at the influence of "Get on the Floor," but Quincy's sound is deeper, as if you're in the eye of a storm—our sound was more like ascending the glass elevator to the top floor while gazing down, rising easily.

Jackie and Randy wrote "Time Waits for No One" with my voice and style in mind. They knew they had to stay up with the Off the Wall songwriters, and they did an excellent job. "Give It Up" allowed everyone a chance to sing, especially Marlon. On those tracks, we drifted from the band sound, possibly falling back into the Philly trap of letting the arrangement overpower us. "Walk Right Now" and "Wondering Who" were closer to the Destiny sound, but they suffered from too many cooks and not enough broth for the most part.

One exception was "Heartbreak Hotel." I swear that sentence came out of my head and I wasn't thinking of any other song at the time. Because of the Elvis Presley connection, the record company placed it on the cover as "This Place Hotel." As important as he was to music, both black and white, he was not an impact on me. He was perhaps too early for me. Perhaps it was more a matter of timing than anything else. By the time our song was released, people believed that if I continued to live in seclusion the way I was, I would die like he did. The comparisons don't exist in my opinion, and I've never been a fan of scare tactics. Still, the manner in which Elvis destroyed himself fascinates me, since I never want to traverse those grounds myself.

LaToya was requested to contribute the opening scream—not the best start to a music career, to be sure, but she was only getting her feet wet in the studio. She has since released some good records and is pretty competent. The scream would ordinarily break a bad dream, but we wanted the dream to only begin, leaving the listener to wonder whether it was a dream or reality. That's what I believe we received. When the three female support vocalists were doing the spooky backup effects that I intended, they were amused until they heard them in the mix.

"Heartbreak Hotel" was my most ambitious tune to date. I believe I operated on several levels: you could dance to it, sing along with it, be horrified by it, and simply listen to it. To comfort the listener, I included a calm piano and cello coda that finished on a good note; there's no use in scaring someone if there's nothing to bring them back safe and sound from where you've taken them. "Heartbreak Hotel" featured revenge, and the thought of revenge fascinates me. It's something I'm not sure of. Making someone "pay" for anything they've done to you or that you believe they've done to you is completely foreign to me. The setting exposed my worries and, for the time being, helped to alleviate them. There were a lot of sharks out there seeking blood in the water.

If this song, and subsequently "Billie Jean," appeared to portray women negatively, it was not intended to be regarded as a personal comment. Needless to say, I enjoy sex interaction; it is a natural aspect of life, and I adore ladies. I simply believe that using sex as a means of extortion or power is a repulsive use of one of God's gifts.

Triumph provided us with the final burst of energy we needed to pull together a flawless presentation with no filler material. We started practising with our touring band, which featured bassist Mike McKinney. David Williams would accompany us on our journeys as well, but he was now a permanent member of the band.

The next tour would be a major undertaking. The legendary magician Doug Henning arranged amazing special effects for us. I wanted to vanish in a burst of smoke right after "Don't Stop." He had to coordinate the special effects with the Showco personnel who were in charge of the entire setup. I was delighted to converse with him while we went about our business. It seemed almost unjust for him to give me his secrets, especially since I wasn't offering him anything in exchange other than money. I was embarrassed, but I truly wanted our concert to be outstanding, and I knew Henning's contribution would be spectacular. We were contending for the position of top band in the country with bands like Earth, Wind, and Fire and the Commodores, and we knew there were those who thought the Jackson brothers had been there for ten years and were done.

I had spent a long time developing the concept for the upcoming tour's set. It had a Close Encounters vibe to it. I was attempting to assert that there was life and significance beyond space and time, and the peacock had sprung forth ever brighter and prouder. I wanted our film to convey this concept as well.

My delight in the rhythms, technological innovations, and success of Off the Wall was mitigated by the shock of hearing the 1979 Grammy nominees. Despite being one of the year's most popular records, Off the Wall only garnered one nomination: Best R&B Vocal Performance. I recall where I was when I heard the news. It stung to feel disregarded by my classmates. People later told me that it surprised the industry as well.

I was sad at first, but then I became enthusiastic about the upcoming album. I told myself, "Wait until next time"—the next album won't be ignored. I watched the ceremony on television, and while it was good to win in my category, I was nonetheless hurt by what I felt as my colleagues' rejection. I kept telling myself, "Next time, next time." An artist is, in many ways, his work. It's difficult to distinguish between the two. I believe I can be ruthlessly objective about my work as it is being created, and if something doesn't work, I can feel it, but when I turn in a full album—or song—you can be sure that I've given it every ounce of energy and God-given talent that I have. Off the Wall was highly welcomed by my fans, which is why the Grammy nominations sting. That encounter ignited a spark in my soul. I couldn't stop thinking about the next record and what I was going to do with it. I wanted it to be genuinely outstanding.

# Chapter 5: The Moonwalk

Off the Wall was published in August 1979, the same month I turned twenty-one and seized control of my own affairs, and it was unquestionably one of the most significant events in my life. It meant a lot to me since it demonstrated beyond a doubt that a former "child star" could evolve into a recording artist with contemporary appeal. Off the Wall also moved beyond the dancing grooves we'd created. Quincy and I discussed how crucial it was to capture passion and strong feelings in a recorded performance when we first started the project. I still believe we accomplished this on the song "She's Out of My Life," and to a lesser extent on "Rock with You."

During the Thriller production, I became angry or upset because I couldn't get the individuals working with me to see what I saw. That still happens to me on occasion. People frequently fail to see what I see. They are filled with scepticism. When you doubt yourself, you can't give your all. Who will believe in you if you don't? Simply repeating your performance from the previous time is insufficient. It's what I call the "Try to get what you can" approach. It does not necessitate you stretching or growing. That is not something I believe in.

I believe we are powerful, but we do not use our minds to their maximum potential. Your mind is powerful enough to assist you in achieving everything you desire. I had an idea for what we could accomplish with that record. We had a terrific team, a lot of skill and amazing ideas, and I thought we could accomplish anything. The popularity of Thriller made many of my fantasies come true. It did become the best-selling album of all time, and the achievement was commemorated on the cover of The Guinness Book of World Records.

Making the Thriller album was a lot of labour, but you only get out of something what you put into it. I'm a perfectionist who will work until I'm exhausted. And I worked quite hard on that CD. Quincy's faith in what we were doing during those sessions aided us. I guess I had proven myself to him throughout our Off the Wall project. He listened to what I had to say and helped me achieve my goals for that album, but he showed even more faith in me throughout the production of Thriller. He understood I had the confidence and experience I needed to do that record, so he wasn't always in the studio with us. When it comes to my work, I'm really confident. When I start on a project, I have complete faith in it. I put my heart and soul into it. I'd give my life for it. That's the way I am.

I had finished several songs of my own, but I didn't submit them to Quincy until I saw what the other writers had sent in. The first song I had was "Startin' Something," which I had written for Off the Wall but never sent to Quincy for that album. Sometimes I write a song that I truly like but can't bring myself to perform it. I even kept "Beat It" for a long period when we were working on Thriller before playing it for Quincy. He kept telling me that the record needed a fantastic rock tune. "Come on, where is it?" he'd remark. "I'm sure you've got it." I like my songs, but I'm hesitant to perform them in front of others because I'm worried they won't like them, which would be a horrible experience.

He eventually persuaded me to let him hear what I had to say. I pulled out "Beat It" and played it for him, and he went absolutely berserk. I felt like I was on top of the world.

Quincy and I eventually settled on "The Girl Is Mine" as Thriller's obvious first single. We didn't have much of a choice. When you have two strong names like that on a song, it has to come out first or it will be overplayed and overplayed. We needed to get that out of the way.

When I approached Paul, I wanted to thank him for providing "Girlfriend" to Off the Wall. I created "The Girl Is Mine," which I felt would be perfect for his and my voices collaborating, and we also worked on "Say Say Say," which we would finish later with George Martin, the legendary Beatles producer.

I eventually purchased the ATV music publishing catalogue, which contained many of the famous Lennon-McCartney tunes. Most people don't realise that Paul was the one who first suggested I get into music publishing. I was staying at Paul and Linda's rural home when Paul informed me about his own engagement in music publishing. He handed me a small book with MPL written on the front cover. He smiled as I opened it, knowing that the contents would pique my interest. It held a list of all the songs Paul owned, and he'd been purchasing song rights for a long time. I had never thought about purchasing tunes before. When the ATV music publishing collection, which included many Lennon-McCartney songs, became available for purchase, I decided to place a bid.

I consider myself a musician who also happens to be a businesswoman, and Paul and I had both learned the hard way about business and the value of publishing and royalties, as well as the dignity of composing. Songwriting should be regarded as the bloodstream of popular music. There are no time clocks or quota systems in the creative process; only inspiration and the determination to follow through. When I was sued by someone I'd never heard of for "The Girl Is Mine," I was more than willing to defend myself. Many of my ideas come to me in dreams, which some people believed was a convenient way out, but it's genuine. Being sued for something you didn't do seems to be as much a part of the initiation process in our field as winning amateur night used to be.

We almost adopted the title "Not My Lover" for "Billie Jean" because Q had some reservations about titling the song "Billie Jean," my original title. He was concerned that people would immediately think of tennis player Billie Jean King.

"Beat It" lyrics indicate what I would do if I were in difficulty. Its message, that we should condemn violence, is one in which I strongly believe. It instructs children to be wise and stay out of danger. I'm not saying you should turn the other cheek as someone kicks you in the teeth, but unless your back is against the wall and you have no option, run away before violence erupts. You gain nothing and lose everything if you fight and are killed. You're a loser, and so are the people you care about. That's what "Beat It" is trying to convey. True bravery, in my opinion, is resolving conflicts without a fight and having the insight to make that solution feasible.

The Toto boys presented "Human Nature" to Q, and he and I both felt that it had the finest melody we'd heard in a long time, even more than "Africa." It's music that has wings. People questioned the words, asking, "Why does he do me that way...?" "I enjoy loving in this manner..." People frequently assume that the lyrics you're singing have some special personal significance for you, which isn't always the case. It is critical to reach out to individuals and move them. This can be done with the mosaic of music melody arrangement and lyrics, or with the intellectual content of the words. I was bombarded with inquiries regarding "Muscles," the song I wrote and produced for Diana Ross. That song fulfilled a lifetime ambition of mine to repay some of the numerous favours she has done for me. Diana has always been a role model for me. My snake's name is Muscles, by the way.

"The Lady in My Life" was one of the most challenging songs to record. We were used to completing a lot of takes to get a vocal as close to perfect as possible, but even after dozens of takes, Quincy wasn't satisfied with my performance on that song. Finally, late one session, he pulled me aside and told me he wanted me to beg. That's exactly what he said. He wanted me to return to the studio and practically beg for it. So I went back in and asked that the studio lights be turned off and the curtain between the studio and the control room be closed so I wouldn't feel self-conscious. I begged Q to stop the tape. What you hear in the grooves is the end outcome.

Our record business eventually put us under immense pressure to finish Thriller. When a record label pushes you, they really rush you, and they rushed us hard on Thriller. They stated it had to be finished by a specific date or else.

So we went through a phase where we were literally hurting our backs to finish the album before the deadline. There were several sacrifices made on the mixes of certain tracks, as well as whether certain tracks would even be included on the album. We cut so many corners that we nearly ruined the album.

When we eventually got down to listening to the tunes we were intending to submit, Thriller sounded so bad that it brought tears to my eyes. We were under immense pressure because, in addition to trying to finish Thriller, we were simultaneously working on The E.T. Storybook, which had a deadline as well. All of these folks were arguing with each other, and we realised that the sad truth was that the Thriller mixes didn't work.

Because I knew it was incorrect. The record would have been catastrophic if we hadn't paused the process and reviewed what we were doing. It would never have been evaluated the way it was because, as we know, a fantastic album can be ruined in the mix. It's like taking a beautiful film and spoiling it in post-production. All you have to do is take your time.

Some things simply cannot be rushed.

The record people yelled and screamed a little, but in the end, they were wise and understood. They were aware as well; it was simply that I was the first to express it. Finally, I realised I had to redo the entire process—mixing the entire album—from scratch.

It felt great when we were done. I couldn't wait for it to come out because I was so eager. There was no celebration when we concluded, as far as I recall. We didn't go to a disco or anything like that. We simply rested. In any case, I'd rather be with folks I care about. That is how I celebrate.

I interviewed several filmmakers for the first video, "Billie Jean," seeking for someone who seemed truly unusual. The majority of them did not present me with anything truly novel. At the same time as I was attempting to imagine bigger, the record business was throwing me a budget dilemma. So I paid for "Beat It" and "Thriller" since I didn't want to quarrel about money with anyone. As a result, I own both of those flicks.

"Billie Jean" was made with money provided by CBS—roughly $250,000. That was a lot of money for a video at the time, but it meant a lot to me that they believed in me that much. Steve Baron, who directed "Billie Jean," had many creative ideas, albeit he wasn't first certain that there should be dance in it. I had the impression that they wanted to witness dancing. It was a lot of fun dancing for the video. Many of the manoeuvres, like the freeze-frame in which I stand on my toes, were spontaneous.

"Billie Jean's" video made a tremendous impression on the MTV audience and was a huge smash.

When I returned to Los Angeles, I saw Bob Giraldi's demo reel and knew he was the man I wanted to direct "Beat It." I liked the way he conveyed stories in his work, so I approached him about "Beat It." We talked about it, my thoughts and his ideas, and that's how it came to be. We manipulated the storyboard by moulding and sculpting it.

When I composed "Beat It," I had street gangs in mind, so we gathered some of Los Angeles' strongest gangs and set them to work on the video. It turned out to be an excellent concept and a fantastic learning experience for me. We had some nasty, tough kids on that set who hadn't been to the wardrobe. Those men in the pool room in the first scene were not performers; they were sincere. That was the real deal.

I hadn't spent much time among tough people before, and these guys were a touch daunting at first. But we had security on hand and were prepared for anything. Of course, we quickly learned that none of this was necessary, since the gang members were usually humble, kind, and friendly in their interactions with us. During breaks, we fed them, and they all cleaned up and put their trays away. I came to know that the whole point of being bad and tough is to gain attention. These individuals had always wanted to be seen and appreciated, and now we were going to put them on television. It was a hit with them. "Hey, look at me, I'm somebody!" And I believe that is why many of the gangs act the way they do. They're rebels, yet they want to be noticed and respected. They, like the rest of us, simply want to be noticed. And I gave them the opportunity. For a few days, they were celebrities.

By the spring of 1983, it was obvious that the record was going to be a smash hit. Out of this world. Every time they launched a new single, LP sales increased even more.

On May 16, 1983, in commemoration of Motown's 25th anniversary, I performed "Billie Jean" on a network transmission. That show was seen by about fifty million people. Many things changed after that.

I found a black jacket during the Thriller sessions and told myself, "You know, someday I'm going to wear this to perform." I wore it on Motown 25 because it was so gorgeous and showy.

But I still had no idea what I was going to do with my solo number the night before the taping. So I went down to our kitchen and played "Billie Jean." Loud. I was alone there the night before the event, and

I basically stood there and let the song tell me what to do. I kind of let the dancing come to me. I truly let it speak to me; when I heard the beat, I took this spy's hat and began to pose and stride, allowing the "Billie Jean" rhythm to produce the movements. I almost felt forced to let things happen on their own. I couldn't help myself. And being able to "step back" and let the dance flow was a lot of joy.

I had also practised specific steps and movements, albeit the most of the performance was spontaneous. I'd been rehearsing the Moonwalk for a while when it occurred to me in our kitchen that I'd finally do it in public on Motown 25.

The Moonwalk was already on the street at this point, but I improved it slightly when I performed it. It began as a break-dance step, a "popping" type of thing invented by black adolescents dancing on street corners in the ghetto. Black people are highly innovative dancers; they invent many of the new dances. So I said to myself, "This is my chance to do it," and I did it. It was taught to me by these three children. They taught me the fundamentals, which I had been practising in private. I had practised it along with a few other steps. All I knew was that on the bridge to "Billie Jean," I was going to go backwards and forwards at the same time, as if I were walking on the moon.

Motown was running late on the day of the taping. Late. So I walked off to practise by myself. I'd already donned my spy helmet. My brothers were curious about the headgear, but I told them they'd have to wait and see.

So, after my brothers and I had completed performing, I approached the side of the platform and remarked, "You're wonderful! I'd like to claim those were the good old days, when I could spend time with all of my brothers, including Jermaine. But what I truly like"—and Nelson is sliding the hat into my hand—"are the latest songs." I spun around, grabbed the hat, and launched into "Billie Jean," into that strong pace; I could see the audience was loving my performance. My brothers told me they were crammed into the wings, mouths open, watching me, and my parents and sisters were in the audience. But I recall opening my eyes at the end and seeing a sea of people getting up and clapping. And I was overcome with contradictory emotions. I knew I had done my best and felt fantastic. At the same time, I was dissatisfied with myself. I had intended to do one long spin and then pause on my toes, suspended for a time, but I didn't stay on my toes as long as I had hoped. I spun around and fell on one toe. I wanted to just stay there, freeze there, but things didn't go as planned.

When I returned onstage, everyone was congratulating me. I was still dissatisfied with the spin. I was concentrating so hard since I am a perfectionist. At the same time, I was aware that this was one of the happiest times of my life. I knew that for the first time, my brothers had a chance to properly observe me and notice what I was doing and how I was changing. Backstage after the show, they all hugged and kissed me. They had never done anything like that before, and I was overjoyed for all of us. It felt so good when they kissed me like that. It was fantastic! We hug all the time, after all. Except for my father, my entire family embraces a lot. He is the sole exception. When the rest of us saw each other, we embraced, but when they all kissed me that night, it seemed like they had blessed me.

Fred Astaire called me on the phone the day after the Motown 25 event. "You're a hell of a mover," he added emphatically. Last night, you really put them on their backsides." That is what Fred Astaire told me. I expressed my gratitude to him. "You're an angry dancer," he continued. I'm in the same boat. That's what I used to do with my cane."

I'd met him a few times before, but this was the first time he'd ever phoned me. "I watched the special last night; I taped it, and I watched it again this morning," he continued. You're a natural dancer."

It was the best compliment I'd ever received, and the only one I'd ever wanted to believe. It meant more to me than anything else for Fred Astaire to tell me that. My performance was later nominated for an Emmy Award in the musical category, but I was defeated by Leontyne Price. It didn't make a difference. That was my reward: Fred Astaire had told me things I'd never forget. Later, he invited me to his place, where he lavished me with additional compliments until I burst out laughing. He meticulously examined my "Billie Jean" performance. Hermes Pan, the brilliant choreographer who had created Fred's dances in the movies, came over, and I showed them how to Moonwalk as well as some other movements that piqued their curiosity.

My family read a lot of publicity about me becoming "the new Sinatra" and "exciting as Elvis" right after Motown 25. It was good to hear, but I knew the press was fickle. They love you one week and treat you like garbage the next.

Later, I sent Sammy Davis the sparkly black jacket I wore on Motown 25 as a gift. He said he was going to perform a takeoff on stage with me, and I asked, "Here, do you want to wear this when you do it?" He was overjoyed. I adore Sammy. He's a wonderful dude and a true showman. One of the very best.

I'd been wearing the glove for a long time, but it didn't get any notice until Michael Jackson released Thriller in 1983. I wore it on several of the old tours back in the 1970s, and I wore it on the Off the Wall tour and on the cover of the live record that followed.

I admit that I enjoy initiating trends, but I never imagined that wearing white socks would become popular. Wearing white socks was once considered exceedingly conservative. It was stylish in the 1950s, but you wouldn't be caught dead wearing white socks in the

1960s and 1970s. For most people, it was too square to even consider.

If fashion says it's not allowed, I'm going to do it.

I don't like to dress up when I'm at home. I wear whatever I can get my hands on. I used to spend entire days in my pjs. I enjoy flannel shirts, vintage sweaters and pants, and uncomplicated clothing.

When I go out, I dress sharper, brighter, and more fitted, but at home and in the studio, anything goes. I don't wear much jewellery, if any at all, because it gets in my way. People occasionally give me jewellery as gifts, and I treasure them for the sentiment, but I usually just store them somewhere. Some of it was taken. Jackie Gleason gave me a lovely ring. He removed it from his finger and handed it to me. It was stolen, and I miss it, but that doesn't worry me since the gesture meant more to me than anything else, and it can never be taken away from me. The ring was just a piece of jewellery.

What truly brings me joy, what I adore, is performing and creating. I'm not interested in the material trappings. I enjoy putting my heart and soul into something and having people accept and like it. That's a lovely sensation.

That is why I enjoy art. I adore Michelangelo and the way he poured his heart into his work. He knew in his heart that he would die one day, but that the work he had done would live on. You can tell he put his heart and soul into painting the ceiling of the Sistine Chapel. He even destroyed everything and started over because he wanted it to be flawless. He went on to say, "If the wine is sour, pour it out."

I can become completely absorbed in a painting. All the pathos and drama draws you in. It converses with you. You can tell what the artist was thinking. I have the same feelings about photography. A powerful or moving photograph can say a lot.

So we reached out to John Landis and asked him to direct. We began work after he agreed and supplied his budget. The technical aspects of this picture were so impressive that I received a call from John Branca, my attorney and one of my closest and most valuable advisers, shortly after. John had been working with me since the Off the Wall days, and he even helped me out by wearing multiple hats and serving in multiple positions when Thriller was out, when I didn't have a manager. He's one of those exceptionally gifted and capable men who can do anything. Anyway, John was in a panic because it was clear that the planned budget for the "Thriller" video would more than double. I was paying for this project myself, therefore the budget overruns were from my own pocket.

But at this time, John had a brilliant idea. He recommended that we film a separate video about the creation of the "Thriller" video, which would be funded by someone else. It seemed strange that no one had done this previously. We were confident that it would be an entertaining documentary that would help pay for our doubled budget. This agreement came together quickly for John. He secured funding from MTV and the Showtime cable network, and Vestron released the video after "Thriller" premiered.

The success of The Making of Thriller surprised all of us. It sold approximately a million cassettes on its own. Even today, it remains the best-selling music video of all time.

The film "Thriller" was completed in late 1983. We published it in February, and it premiered on MTV. When Epic released "Thriller" as a single, LP sales skyrocketed. According to statistics, the introduction of the "Thriller" film and song resulted in fourteen million increased album and tape sales in a six-month period. We were selling a million records per week at one time in 1984.

This response continues to astound me. When we eventually ended the Thriller campaign a year later, the album had sold 32 million copies. Today's revenues total forty million. A dream realised.

During this time, I also changed my management. In early 1983, my contract with Weisner and DeMann expired. My father no longer represented me, and I was searching about. I was seeing Frank Dileo at the Beverly Hills Hotel one day when I asked him if he was interested in quitting Epic and managing my career.

Frank urged me to think about it some more and to contact him back on Friday if I was certain.

Needless to say, I returned the call.

Thriller's success truly hit me in 1984, when the album garnered a slew of nominations for American Music Awards and Grammy Awards. I recall experiencing an exhilarating burst of joy. I was yelling and whooping with joy throughout the home. I couldn't believe it when the album was named the best-selling album of all time. "Bust open the champagne!" exclaimed Quincy Jones. We were all in a bad mood. Man! What a sensation! To put forth so much effort, to offer so much, and to achieve! Everyone participating in Thriller seemed to be floating on air. It was fantastic.

I pictured myself feeling like a long-distance runner breaking the tape at the finish line. I imagine an athlete sprinting as hard and as quickly as he can. Finally, he draws close to the finish line and his chest hits the ribbon, sending the audience into a frenzy. And I'm not even a sports fan!

But I can relate to that individual because I know how hard he's worked and how much that moment means to him. Perhaps an entire life has been devoted to this one moment. Then he triumphs. That is the fulfilment of a dream. That's some serious power. I can relate because I understand.

One of the side consequences of the Thriller period was that I became tired of being in the public eye all the time. As a result, I vowed to live a quieter, more private life. I was still self-conscious about my appearance. You must remember that I was a child star, and when you grow up under such scrutiny, no one wants you to change, to get older, and to appear different. I had a lot of baby fat and a plump, chubby face when I first became famous. That roundness persisted with me until I changed my diet and quit eating beef, poultry, pork, and fish, as well as other fattening foods, several years ago. I simply desired to appear better, live better, and be healthier. As I dropped weight, my face gradually took on its current shape, and the press began accusing me of surgically modifying my appearance beyond the nose job I readily confessed I had, as do many other performers and film stars. They would compare an old photograph from youth or high school to a recent photograph. My face would be fat and flabby in the old picture. I'd have an Afro, and the photo would be dark. The new photograph would depict a much older, more mature face. I have a different nose and a different hairdo. In addition, the lighting in the current images is great. Making such comparisons is simply not fair. They claim I underwent bone surgery on my face. People jumping to that conclusion seemed unusual to me, and I thought it was really unfair.

Many celebrities, including Judy Garland and Jean Harlow, have undergone nose jobs. My issue is that as a child celebrity, people became accustomed to seeing me appear one way.

I'd like to correct the record right now. I've never had my cheeks or my eyes altered. I've never had my lips thinned or had dermabrasion or a skin peel. All of these charges are absurd. I would say so if they were true, but they aren't. My nose has been changed twice, and I recently added a cleft to my chin, but that is all. Period. Whatever everyone else says, it's my face, and I know.

I'm a vegetarian now, and I've lost a lot of weight. For years, I've been on a rigorous diet. I am healthier and more energised than I have ever been. I'm not sure why the press is so preoccupied with my appearance in the first place. What does my facial expression have to do with my music or dancing?

A man recently asked me if I was content. "I don't think I'll ever be completely happy," I replied. I'm one of the most difficult people to please, but I'm also conscious of how much I have to be thankful for, and I'm grateful for my health and the affection of my family and friends.

I'm also easily humiliated. On the network broadcast the night I won eight American Music Awards, I accepted them while wearing my shades. Katharine Hepburn called and thanked me, but she chastised me for wearing sunglasses. "Your fans want to see your eyes," she chastised. "You're cheating them." The next month, in February 1984, at the Grammy Awards, Thriller had gone away with seven Grammy Awards and appeared to be on its way to an eighth. I'd been coming up to the podium and collecting awards with my sunglasses all evening. Finally, when Thriller won Best Album, I went up to accept the award, removed my spectacles, and stared into the camera. "Katharine Hepburn," she responded, "this is for you." I had a feeling she was watching, and she was.

You must have some fun.

# Chapter 6: All You Need Is Love

I had intended to spend the majority of 1984 working on some film ideas I had, but those plans were derailed. First, I was burned on the set of a Pepsi commercial I was filming with my brothers in January.

The fire was started by stupidity, plain and simple. We were filming at night, and I was supposed to descend a stairway with magnesium flash bombs going off on either side and close behind me. It appeared to be so straightforward. I was supposed to walk down the steps while these bombs exploded behind me. We shot numerous takes that were perfectly timed. The bombs' lightning effects were fantastic. Only afterward did I realise that these bombs were only two feet away from either side of my head, which violated all safety standards. I was meant to stand two feet on either side of a magnesium explosion.

The director, Bob Giraldi, then approached me and said, "Michael, you're going down too soon." We'd like to see you up there on the stairs. We want to show your presence when the lights turn on, so please wait."

So I waited, as bombs exploded on either side of my head and sparkles ignited my hair. I was dancing down this ramp, twirling around and spinning, unaware that I was on fire. My hands instinctively went to my head in an attempt to smother the flames. I collapsed and simply tried to shake the flames out. Jermaine turned around and saw me on the ground shortly after the explosions, and he assumed I had been shot by someone in the crowd—we were filming in front of a large audience. That's how it appeared to him.

Miko Brando, a colleague of mine, was the first to contact me. It was anarchy after that. It was insane. No film could adequately convey the intensity of that night. The audience was yelling. "Get some ice!" someone yelled. There was a frenetic rushing noise. "Oh no!"

exclaimed the crowd. Before they put me in the ambulance, I noticed the Pepsi executives gathered together in a corner, afraid. I recall the medical personnel placing me on a cot and the Pepsi guys being so terrified that they couldn't even bring themselves to check on me.

Despite the excruciating discomfort, I remained disconnected. I was watching the whole thing develop. They later told me I was in shock, but I remember enjoying the ride to the hospital since I never imagined myself riding in an ambulance with sirens blaring. It was one of those things I had always wanted to do as a kid. When we arrived, they informed me that there were television crews outside, so I requested my glove. There's a famous photo of me waving from the stretcher while wearing my glove.

One of the physicians later informed me that it was a marvel I was still alive. One of the firefighters remarked that in most cases, your clothing catches fire, and your entire face can be scarred or you can die. That's all. I had third-degree burns on the back of my head that almost went through to my skull, so I had a lot of issues, but I was quite fortunate.

We now know that the incident generated a lot of attention for the commercial. They sold the most Pepsi in history. They eventually returned to me and gave me the largest commercial endorsement pay in history. It was so unusual that it was inscribed in the Guinness Book of World Records. Pepsi and I collaborated on another commercial, "The Kid," and I caused havoc by limiting the shots of me since I felt the shots they wanted didn't work properly. They later told me I was correct after the commercial was a success.

I recall how terrified the Pepsi executives appeared the night of the fire. They reasoned that my being burned would leave a sour taste in the mouths of all Pepsi-drinking kids in America. They were aware that I could have sued them, and I could have, but I was quite polite about it. Very great. They awarded me $1,500,000, which I donated right away to the Michael Jackson Burn Center. I wanted to do something because the other burn patients I met in the hospital moved me.

Then came the Victory Tour. Over the course of five months, I performed at fifty-five gigs with my brothers.

I refused to go on the Victory Tour and battled against it. I felt it would be best for me not to do the tour, but my brothers insisted, so I did it for them. So I told myself that if I was going to do this, I may as well put my heart and soul into it.

When it came to the real tour, I was outvoted on a number of matters, but you don't worry about that when you're onstage. My goal for the Victory Tour was to give every performance my all. I hoped that people who didn't even like me would come to see me. I was hoping they'd hear about the show and want to see what was going on. I wanted an excellent word-of-mouth response to the play so that a diverse spectrum of individuals could come see us. Word of mouth is the most effective form of advertising. Nothing compares. I'm sold if someone I trust tells me something is fantastic.

During the Victory Days, I felt extremely powerful. I felt like I was on top of the world. I was fired up. "We're a mountain," said the tour guide. We've come to show you our music. "We have something to tell you." We rose from the stage and down these stairs at the start of the concert. The beginning was dramatic and bright, and it perfectly conveyed the mood of the event. When the lights came on and they saw us, the roof would fall in.

It felt good to be playing with my brothers again. It allowed us to recapture our glory days as the Jackson 5 and the Jacksons. We were all back together. Jermaine had returned, and we were riding a tide of success. It was the largest tour any band had ever done, with massive outdoor stadiums. However, I was dissatisfied with the tour from the start. I wanted to move the globe in ways it had never been moved before. I wanted to deliver something that made people say, "Wow! That's wonderful!" The feedback we received was fantastic, and the people were fantastic, but I became dissatisfied with our show. I didn't have the time or opportunity to perfect it as much as I would have liked. I was let down by the staging of "Billie Jean." I had hoped it would be so much more. I didn't like the lighting, and I never got my steps exactly right. It hurt me to accept these things and settle for doing things the way I did.

There have been moments when specific things bothered me just before a show—business or personal issues. "I don't know how to go through with this," I thought. I'm not sure how I'll get through the show. I can't keep up like this."

But something happens when I get to the edge of the stage. The rhythm begins, and the lights hit me, and the problems fade away. This has happened numerous times. The excitement of performing simply takes over. It's as if God is saying, "Yes, you can." You certainly can. Simply wait. Just wait till you hear this. Just wait until you see this." And the backbeat penetrates into my backbone, vibrates, and simply takes me. When I almost lose control, the musicians ask, "What is he doing?" and begin following me. You alter the entire scheduling of a piece. You come to a halt and begin again, doing something completely different. The tune sends you somewhere else.

On the Victory tour, there was a section of the show when I was doing this scattering theme and the audience was repeating everything I said. "Da, de, da, de," I'd say, and they'd reply, "Da, de, da, de." When I've done it in the past, they've started stomping. When the entire audience does this, it sounds like an earthquake. Oh! It's a terrific feeling to be able to do that with all those people—who are all doing the same thing you are. It's the most wonderful sensation in the world. When you glance around the crowd, you see toddlers, teens, grandparents, and adults in their twenties and thirties. Everyone is moving, raising their hands, and singing. You request that the house lights be turned on so you can see their faces. You say, "Hold hands," and they do, then you say, "Stand up" or "Clap," and they do. They're having a good time and will do whatever you tell them. They adore it, and it's so great to see people of all ethnicities doing it together. "Look around you," I remark at such moments. Take a look at yourself. Look. Take a look around you. Take a look at what you've done." Oh, it's so lovely. Very strong. Those are fantastic moments.

The Victory tour was my first opportunity to interact with Michael Jackson fans since Thriller two years prior. There were some odd reactions. I'd run into individuals in the corridors who'd say, "Naw, that can't be him." He wouldn't be present." I was perplexed, and I kept asking myself, "Why wouldn't I?" I'm someplace on the planet. I have to be somewhere at all times. "Why not right here?" Some admirers believe you're a phantom, a thing that doesn't exist. They think you're a miracle or something when they see you. Fans have asked if I use the restroom. It becomes awkward. Because they are so enthusiastic, they lose sight of the fact that you are similar to them. But I understand because I would have felt the same way if I had met Walt Disney or Charlie Chaplin.

The tour kicked off in Kansas City. Victory was having her first night out. In the evening, we were walking by the hotel pool when Frank Dileo lost his balance and fell in. People became excited when they noticed this. Some of us were blushing, but I was laughing. He wasn't wounded, and he appeared shocked. We leaped over a short wall and ended up on the street with no security. People didn't seem to believe we were just strolling down the street like that. They gave us plenty of room.

When we got back to the hotel, Bill Bray, who has been in charge of my security team since I was a child, just shook his head and laughed as we told him about our exploits.

Bill is meticulous and professional in his work, but he isn't concerned with what happens after the fact. He travels everywhere with me and is sometimes my only companion on short excursions. I can't picture my existence without Bill; he's friendly, amusing, and completely enamoured with life. He's a wonderful man.

I was out on our hotel balcony with Frank, who has a terrific sense of humour and enjoys performing pranks himself, when the tour was in Washington, D.C. We were tormenting each other when I began removing $100 dollars from his pockets and tossing them to folks walking down below. This almost resulted in a riot. He was attempting to dissuade me, but we were both giggling. It reminded me of the jokes my brothers and I used to play while on tour. Frank dispatched our security personnel downstairs to search for any undiscovered money in the bushes.

During the four-block journey from the hotel to the stadium in Jacksonville, local cops nearly killed us in a traffic accident. Later, in another section of Florida, when the usual tour ennui set in, I performed a little trick on Frank. I invited him to my suite, and when he entered, I offered him some watermelon that was on a table across the room. Frank rushed over to get a piece and stumbled over Muscles, my boa constrictor, who was riding with me. Muscles are harmless, but Frank despises snakes and screams and yells. With the boa, I began chasing him around the room. Frank, on the other hand, had the upper hand. He became terrified, bolted from the room, and seized the security guard's revolver. He was about to shoot Muscles when the guard intervened. Later, he stated that all he could think about was "I've got to get that snake." I've discovered that many macho men are terrified of snakes.

We were imprisoned in hotels around the United States, exactly like in the old days. We'd get up to our old pranks, grabbing buckets of water and pouring them down hotel balconies onto people eating in the atriums far below. We were so far up that the water had turned to mist by the time it reached them. It was precisely like the old days: bored in hotels, separated from fans for our own safety, and unable to leave without extensive security.

But there were plenty of enjoyable days as well. We had a lot of free time on that trip, and we got to go to Disney World five times. An extraordinary incident happened once while we were staying at the hotel there. It's something I'll never forget. I was on a balcony from where we could see a large area. There were so many people. People were colliding with one another because it was so crowded. Someone in the crowd recognized me and began yelling my name. Thousands of people began yelling, "Michael! Michael!" which echoed throughout the park. The chanting continued until it became so loud that ignoring it would have been impolite. Everyone started yelling as soon as I did. "Oh, this is so lovely," I exclaimed. "I'm so talented." All of my efforts on Thriller, all of my tears and believing in my dreams and labouring on those songs and falling asleep near the microphone stand because I was so fatigued, were repaid by this demonstration of affection.

I've walked into a theatre to see a play and everyone immediately starts cheering. Simply because they are relieved that I am present. I feel honoured and thrilled at times like that. It makes all of the effort worthwhile.

The Victory tour was initially titled "The Final Curtain" since we all realised it would be our final tour together. But we opted against emphasising it.

The excursion was enjoyable for me. I knew it would be a long path, and it was probably too lengthy in the end. For me, the finest part was witnessing the children in the audience. Every night, there would be a group of people who had dressed up. They were ecstatic. The youngsters on the tour, of various ethnicities and ages, greatly motivated me. It's been my desire since I was a child to bring people from all over the world together through love and music. I still feel goosebumps every time I hear the Beatles perform "All You Need Is Love." I've always dreamed that this song could be a global anthem.

I enjoyed the shows we performed in Miami and the time we spent there. Colorado was also fantastic. We were able to spend some time relaxing at Caribou Ranch. And, as always, New York was spectacular. Emmanuel Lewis attended the event, as did Yoko, Sean Lennon, Brooke, and many other close friends. In retrospect, the offstage moments stand out just as much as the concerts themselves. I discovered that I could lose myself in some of those shows. I recall swinging my jackets around and hurling them into the crowd. The wardrobe folks would become irritated with me, and I'd honestly say, "I'm sorry, but I can't help myself." I can't stop myself. Something takes over, and I know I shouldn't do it, but you can't help yourself. There's a mood of joy and communion that comes over you, and you just want to let it all out."

We found out my sister Janet had married while we were on the Victory tour. Because I am so close to Janet, everyone was hesitant to inform me. I was taken aback. I am quite protective of her. Quincy Jones's daughter was the one who told me the news.

I've always had a fantastically close relationship with all three of my lovely sisters. LaToya is an exceptional individual. She's really pleasant to be around, but she can also be rather amusing. You enter her room and are unable to sit on the couch, sit on the bed, or walk on the carpet. This is the reality. She'll chase you out of her room. She wants everything in there to be perfect. "You have to walk on the carpet sometimes," I say, but she doesn't want prints on it. She covers her plate if you cough at the table. If you sneeze, you're out. That's the way she is. Mother claims she used to be the same way.

Janet, on the other hand, was a tomboy from the start. For the longest time, she has been my family's best friend. That's why it broke my heart to see her get married. Everything was done in collaboration. We have similar interests and a similar sense of humour. When we were younger, we'd get up on "free" mornings and plan out our entire day. GET UP, FEED THE ANIMALS, HAVE BREAKFAST, WATCH SOME CARTOONS, GO TO THE MOVIES, GO TO A RESTAURANT, GO TO ANOTHER MOVIE, GO HOME AND SWIMMING. That was our concept of a wonderful day. We'd go back to the list in the evening and reflect on how much fun we'd had.

It was fantastic to be with Janet since we didn't have to worry about either of us not liking things. We had similar tastes. We'd occasionally read to each other. She was like my identical twin.

LaToya and I, on the other hand, are diametrically opposed. She won't even feed the animals since the smell alone turns her off. And don't even think of going to the movies. She has no idea what I see in Star Wars, Close Encounters, or Jaws. Our cinematic tastes are diametrically opposed.

We'd be inseparable when Janet was around and I wasn't working on something. But I knew we'd eventually form our own interests and ties. It was unavoidable.

Unfortunately, her marriage did not last long, but she is now content. Marriage, I believe, can be a great thing if it is right for the two people involved. I believe in love—I mean, how can you not after you've experienced it? Relationships are important to me. I'm sure I'll find the ideal woman and marry one day. I often look forward to having children; in fact, having a large family would be ideal, as I come from a huge one myself. In my fantasy about having a huge family, I have thirteen children.

Right now, my work consumes the majority of my time and

emotions. I'm always working. I enjoy making things and coming up with fresh ideas. In terms of the future, Whatever happens, happens. Only time will tell. It would be difficult for me to be that reliant on others, but I can visualise it if I tried. I have so many things I want to accomplish and so much work to complete.

I can't help but notice some of the criticism directed at me at times. Journalists appear to be eager to say anything to sell a newspaper. They think I've had my eyes enlarged because I want to appear whiter. What about more white? What kind of assertion is that? Plastic surgery was not invented by me. It's been around for quite some time. Many very fine, very pleasant people have undergone plastic surgery. Nobody blogs about their surgery and criticises them like this. It's not right. The vast majority of what they print is a fake. It's enough to make you wonder, "Where did the truth go?" "Did it go out of fashion?"

Finally, the most essential thing is to be true to yourself and people you care about, and to work hard. Work as if there's no tomorrow. Train. Strive. I mean, actually train and grow your talent to the best of your ability. Make yourself the best at what you do. Learn more about your field than anybody else alive. Use your tools, whether they be books, a dance floor, or a body of water to swim in. It's yours, whatever it is. That's what I've always tried to keep in mind. During the Victory Tour, I gave it a lot of thought.

On the Victory tour, I felt like I impacted a lot of people. Not in the way I had hoped, but I figured it would come later, when I was on my own, performing and directing movies. I donated all of my performance money to charity, including donations for the burn centre that assisted me following the Pepsi set fire. That year, we contributed more than $4 million. Giving back was what the Victory Tour was all about for me.

Following my experiences with the Victory Tour, I began making more deliberate career decisions than ever before. I had learnt a lesson on a previous trip, which I clearly remembered throughout the struggles with Victory.

Years ago, we went on a tour with this guy who ripped us off, but he taught me something. "Listen, all these people work for you," he continued. You are not employed by them. You are the one who is paying them."

That's what he kept telling me. Finally, I realised what he was saying. It was a whole new concept for me because everything was done for us at Motown. Our decisions were determined by others. That encounter has left me mentally damaged. "You have to wear this. You must perform these songs. You're coming here. You'll do this interview and that TV show." That's how things went. We were at a loss for words. I eventually awoke when he told me I was in charge. He was correct, I realised.

Regardless, I owe that guy a debt of gratitude.

Captain Eo was created when the Disney Studios asked me to create a new attraction for the parks. They claimed it didn't matter what I did as long as it was innovative. I had this big discussion with them, and during the day I told them that Walt Disney was my hero and that I was really interested in Disney's history and philosophy. I wanted to make something with them that Mr. Disney would be proud of. I'd read a few books on Walt Disney and his creative empire, and it was crucial to me to execute things the way he would have.

Finally, they approached me about doing a film, and I agreed. I told them I wanted to collaborate with George Lucas and Steven Spielberg. Because Steven was unavailable, George enlisted the services of Francis Ford Coppola, and thus the Captain Eo team was formed.

I drove up to San Francisco a few times to meet George at his home, Skywalker Ranch, and eventually we came up with a plot for a short film that would combine every new advancement in 3-D technology. Captain Eo would make the audience feel as if they were passengers on a starship.

Captain Eo is about metamorphosis and the power of music to affect change in the world. Captain Eo was created by George. (Eo is the Greek word meaning "dawn.") The plot revolves around a young man who is sent on a mission to this desolate planet ruled by an evil queen. He is tasked with the task of delivering light and beauty to the population. It's a fantastic celebration of good triumphing over evil.

Working on Captain Eo confirmed all of my favourable thoughts about working in cinema and made me know more than ever that movies are most likely my future career. I've always loved movies and have done so since I was a child. You can be moved to another location for two hours. Films can transport you anywhere. That's what I enjoy. "OK, nothing else exists right now," I can sit down and say. Take me to a great location and make me forget about my pressures, problems, and daily schedule."

I also enjoy working in front of a 35 mm camera. I used to hear my brothers say, "I'll be glad when this shoot is over," and I couldn't figure out why. I'd be watching, trying to figure out what the director was trying to achieve and what the light man was doing. I was curious about the source of the light and why the director was repeating a scenario so many times. I was interested in hearing about the script adjustments. It's all part of what I consider my continual cinematic education. Pioneering new ideas excites me, and the movie industry appears to be suffering from a lack of ideas right now; so many people are doing the same things. The large studios remind me of how Motown acted when we disagreed with them: they wanted easy solutions, they wanted their personnel to do formula stuff—sure bets—but the public became bored, of course. So many of them are repeating themselves. The exceptions are George Lucas and Steven Spielberg.

I'm going to try to make some adjustments. I'm going to try to make some changes someday.

Marlon Brando has become a dear and trustworthy friend of mine. I cannot express how much he has taught me. We could talk for hours. He has informed me a lot about the films. He is a fantastic performer who has worked with numerous industry titans, from other actors to cameramen. He has an amazing appreciation for the creative worth of filmmaking. He's like a father figure to me.

So, these days, movies are my number one dream, but I also have many other dreams.

We recorded "We Are the World" in early 1985 at an all-night all-star recording session organised following the American Music Awards event. After viewing horrifying television pictures of malnourished people in Ethiopia and Sudan, I collaborated with Lionel Richie to write the song.

Around that time, I'd invite my sister Janet to accompany me into a room with unusual acoustics, such as a closet or the bathroom, and I'd sing to her, just a note, a rhythm of a note. I'd just hum from the bottom of my voice, no lyrics or anything. "Janet, what do you see?" I'd ask. When you hear this music, what do you see?" And this time she added, "Dying children in Africa."

"You're correct. That's what my soul was telling me."

"You're talking about Africa," she said. You're talking about children who are dying." That is where the song "We Are the World" came from. We'd go into a dark room and I'd sing her notes. That, in my opinion, is what singers should be able to achieve. Even in a dark room, we should be able to perform and be productive. We've lost a lot because of television. You should be able to move people without using any modern technology, without using pictures, and solely utilising sound.

I've been acting since I can remember. I know a lot of secrets and stuff like that.

"We Are the World" is, in my opinion, a highly spiritual song, but in a unique way. I felt honoured to be a part of that song and one of the musicians who performed that night. Our ambition to make a difference brought us together. It made the world a better place for us, and it helped the needy people we wished to assist.

We got several Grammys and started hearing easy-listening renditions of "We Are the World" and "Billie Jean" in elevators, along with "Billie Jean." I had always imagined the song being performed by children since I originally wrote it. I almost sobbed when I heard youngsters singing it on producer George Duke's rendition. It's the nicest rendition I've ever heard.

After "We Are the World," I chose to withdraw from public view once more. For the next two and a half years, I committed the majority of my time to recording the follow-up to Thriller, Bad.

What took so long to make Bad? Quincy and I agreed that this CD should be as near to perfect as humanly possible. A perfectionist must take his time, shaping, moulding, and sculpting that object until it is flawless. He can't let it go until he's completely satisfied.

If something isn't right, you throw it away and start over. You work on it until it's just right. You put it out there when it's as flawless as you can make it. It's so important to get it precisely perfect; that's the key. That's the difference between a thirty-first-place record and a number-one record that stays at the top for weeks. It has to be good. If it is, it will stay up there, and the entire world will wonder when it will come down.

I'm having trouble expressing how Quincy Jones and I collaborate on a record. I compose the tunes and make the music, and then Quincy brings out the best in me. That is the only way I can put it. Quincy will listen and make adjustments. "Michael, you should put a change in there," he'll suggest, and I'll do so. And he'll guide me and assist me in creating, inventing, and working on new sounds, new types of music.

And we're fighting. We had some disagreements during the Bad sessions. If we have any difficulties, it is with modern technologies. I'll put it this way: "Quincy, you know, music changes all the time." I'm looking for the most recent drum sounds. I want to go beyond the freshest and greatest. Then we go out and make the best record we possibly can.

We never strive to appease the fans. We simply strive to capitalise on the song's quality. People will not buy garbage. They will only buy what they want. You have to genuinely like what you're about to buy if you go to the trouble of getting in your car, driving to the record store, and putting your money on the counter. "I'll put a country song on here for the country market, a rock song for that market," and so on. I am drawn to a wide range of musical styles. I enjoy some rock tunes, some country songs, some pop songs, and all of the old rock 'n' roll records.

We did aim for a rock song with "Beat It." We hired Eddie Van Halen to play guitar because we believed he would do an excellent job. Albums should cater to people of all races and musical inclinations.

Many songs, in the end, make themselves. "This is it," you say. This is how things will be." Of course, not every song will have a good dance beat. It's almost as if "Rock with You" doesn't have a good dancing beat. It was intended for the ancient Rock dance. But it's not a "Don't Stop" or "Working Day and Night" beat or a "Startin'

Somethin'" type of song that you can work out on the dance floor.

We spent a long period working on Bad. Years. It was ultimately worthwhile since we were pleased with the results, but it was also difficult. We were tense because we thought we were competing with ourselves. It's difficult to produce something when you feel like you're competing with yourself because, no matter what, people will always compare Bad to Thriller. "Aw, forget Thriller," you may always say, but no one ever does.

I believe I have a tiny advantage in this situation because I always perform best under pressure.

"Bad" is a song about life on the streets. It's about a poor youngster who gets to attend a prestigious private school. He returns to his old area during a break from school, and the youngsters from the neighbourhood start causing him problems. He says, "I'm bad, you're bad, who's bad, who's the best?" He's suggesting that while you're strong and good, you're also bad.

The message of "Man in the Mirror" is excellent. That music is fantastic. If John Lennon were still alive, he would be able to relate to that song since it emphasises that in order to make the world a better place, you must first work on yourself and change. It's similar to what John F. Kennedy meant when he said, "Ask not what your country can do for you; ask what you can do for your country." Take a look at yourself and make a change if you want to make the world a better place. Begin with yourself in the mirror. Begin with yourself. Don't be distracted by everything else. Begin with yourself.

That is correct. That's what Martin Luther King and Gandhi intended. That is my opinion.

Several folks have asked me if I was thinking about someone in particular when I composed "Can't Stop Loving You." And I truly don't think I did. I was thinking about someone while singing it, but not when writing it.

Except for "Man in the Mirror," which Siedah Garrett wrote with George Ballard, and "Just Good Friends," which is by these two authors who wrote "What's Love Got to Do with It" for Tina Turner, I wrote all of the songs on Bad. We needed a duet for me and Stevie Wonder, and they had this song; I don't think they really intended it to be a duet. They wrote it specifically for me, but I thought it would be wonderful for Stevie and me to sing together.

"Another Part of Me" was one of the first songs composed for Bad, and it made its public appearance at the end of Captain Eo, when the captain bids farewell. "Speed Demon" is a song about machines. "Smooth Criminal" and "The Way You Make Me Feel" are just the grooves I was in at the time. That's how I'd phrase it.

"Leave Me Alone" is a track that can only be found on Bad's compact CD. I laboured long and hard on the tune, stacking vocals on top of each other like clouds. Here's a simple message: "Leave me alone." The song is about a guy and a girl's relationship. But what I truly mean to those who bother me is, "Leave me alone."

The pressure of achievement has an odd effect on people. Many people achieve success rapidly and it is an instant occurrence in their lives. Some of these people, whose achievement may be a one-time occurrence, are unsure how to deal with what happens to them.

Because I've been in this field for so long, I have a distinct view on celebrity. I've learnt that the best way to survive as your own person is to avoid personal publicity and maintain as low a profile as possible. It's probably good in some ways and bad in others.

The most difficult aspect is the lack of privacy. When we were filming "Thriller," Jackie Onassis and Shaye Areheart travelled to California to talk about this book. There were photographers in the trees all over the place. It was impossible for us to act without being observed and reported.

The cost of celebrity can be high. Is the price you pay reasonable? Consider the fact that you have no privacy. You won't be able to accomplish anything unless you make specific arrangements. Whatever you say is printed in the media. They report whatever you do. They know what you buy, what movies you watch, everything. When I visit a public library, they print the titles of the books I borrow. In Florida once, they printed my full schedule in the paper; everything I did from ten in the morning until six at night. "After he did this, he did that, and after he did that, he went there, then he went door to door, and then he ..."

I recall thinking to myself, "What if I were trying to do something that I didn't happen to want reported in the paper?" All of this is the price of fame.

I think my image gets distorted in the public's mind. They don't get a clear or full picture of what I'm like, despite the press coverage I mentioned early. Mistruths are printed as fact, in some cases, and frequently only half of a story will be told. The part that doesn't get printed is often the part that would make the printed part less sensational by shedding light on the facts. As a result, I think some people don't think I'm a person who determines what's happening with his career. Nothing could be further from the truth.

I've been accused of being preoccupied with my privacy, and it's true that I am. When you're famous, everyone looks at you. They are watching you, which is understandable, but it is not always simple. If you were to ask me why I wear sunglasses in public so often, I'd tell you it's because I don't like having to look everyone in the eyes all the time. It's a means of hiding a little piece of myself. After I had my wisdom teeth out, the dentist provided me with a surgical mask to wear at home to keep germs at bay. I adored that mask. It was fantastic—much better than sunglasses—and I had a lot of fun wearing it around for a time. Because I have so little privacy in my life, covering a small bit of myself is a chance for me to get away from it all. I know it's unusual, but I value my privacy.

I'm not sure if I appreciate being famous, but I do enjoy accomplishing goals. I enjoy not only meeting but exceeding goals I set for myself. It's a terrific feeling to have accomplished more than I believed possible. There's nothing else like it. Setting objectives for yourself is crucial in my opinion. It provides you with a notion of where you want to go and how you want to get there. You'll never know if you didn't aim for anything if you don't try.

I've always joked that I didn't ask to sing and dance, but it's true. When I open my mouth, music comes forth. I consider myself fortunate to have this talent. I thank God for it every day. I attempt to grow what He has given me. I feel obliged to do what I do.

There are so many things to be grateful for all around us. Wasn't it Robert Frost who wrote about the globe in a leaf? That appears to be correct. That is what I enjoy most about working with children. They notice everything. They aren't jaded. They get enthused about stuff we've lost interest in. They are also quite natural and unselfconscious. I enjoy being around them. There are always a slew of kids over at the house, and they are always welcome. Being around them energises me. They look at everything with such fresh eyes and open minds. That is part of what makes children so creative. They don't care about the regulations. The image does not have to be in the centre of the piece of paper. The sky does not have to be blue. They, too, are welcoming of others. Their only desire is to be treated fairly—and to be loved. That's what I believe we all want.

I'd like to think that I'm an inspiration to the children I encounter. I want kids to enjoy my music. Their approval matters more to me than anyone else's. It is always the children that predict which song will be a smash. You see kids who can't even talk yet but have a little rhythm going. It's hilarious. However, they are a difficult audience. In fact, they are the most difficult audience. So many parents have come to me and told me that their child knows "Beat It" or "Thriller." George Lucas told me that his daughter's first words were "Michael Jackson." When he said it, I felt like I was on top of the world.

I spend a lot of my free time visiting children's hospitals, both in California and while travelling. It makes me so glad to be able to brighten those kids' days simply by showing up and talking with them, listening to what they have to say, and making them feel better. It's very awful that children have to get sick. Children, more than anyone else, do not deserve it. They frequently have no idea what is wrong with them. It twists my heart. When I'm with them, I simply want to hug them and make everything great for them. Sick youngsters will occasionally visit me at home or at my hotel rooms while I'm on the road. A parent will contact me and ask if their child can come see me for a few minutes. When I'm around them, I get a deeper understanding of what my mother may have gone through with her polio. Life is too precious and too brief not to reach out and touch the people we can.

Kids never let me down when I was going through a hard patch with my skin and adolescent growth spurts. They were the only ones who acknowledged that I was no longer tiny Michael and that I was still the same person on the inside, even if you didn't recognize me. That is something I will never forget. Kids are wonderful. If all I lived for was to help and please children, that would suffice. They're amazing folks. Amazing.

I am a person who is very much in charge of his life. I have a team of fantastic people working for me, and they do an excellent job of presenting me with the data that keeps me up to date on everything that's going on at MJJ Productions so that I can know the possibilities and make the judgments. My creativity is my realm, and I appreciate it as much as or more than any other element of my life.

I think I have a goody-goody image in the press, which I despise, but it's difficult to combat because I don't generally talk about myself. I am a shy person. It's true. I dislike doing interviews or appearing on talk shows. When Doubleday approached me about writing this book, I was excited about the prospect of being able to express myself in a book that would be entirely mine—my words and my voice. I hope it helps to dispel some myths.

Everybody, including myself, has multiple sides. When I'm out in public, I'm often shy and quiet. Obviously, I feel differently when I'm not surrounded by cameras and people staring at me. My friends and close associates are aware that there is another Michael who I find difficult to present in the bizarre "public" situations in which I frequently find myself.

But it's different when I'm onstage. I lose myself when I perform. That stage is completely under my control. I'm not thinking about anything. I know exactly what I want to accomplish from the time I walk out the door, and I enjoy every minute of it. Onstage, I'm actually calm. I'm completely at ease. It's lovely. I'm also at ease in the studio. I can tell whether something feels correct. If it doesn't, I know how to make it work. Everything must be in order for you to feel good and fulfilled. People used to underestimate my songwriter abilities. They didn't think of me as a songwriter, so when I started writing songs, they'd ask, "Who really wrote that?" I'm not sure what they must have thought—that I had someone writing them for me out in the garage? But, as time passed, those assumptions were dispelled. You always have to prove yourself to people, and many of them are sceptical. I've heard stories of Walt Disney going from studio to studio, unsuccessfully trying to sell his work and being turned down. Everyone felt he was the greatest thing that had ever happened when he was finally given a chance.

When you are treated unfairly, it might make you stronger and more determined. Slavery was a terrible thing, but when black people in

America were eventually free of it, they were stronger. They understood what it was like to have your spirit stifled by individuals in charge of your life. They would never let that happen again. That kind of bravery inspires me. People who have it take a position and pour their hearts and souls into their beliefs.

People frequently inquire about my personality. I'm hoping that this book will answer some of those questions, but these may also be useful. My favourite music is a diverse combination. For instance, I enjoy classical music. Debussy is one of my favourite composers. Prelude to a Faun's Afternoon with Clair de Lune. Also, Prokofiev. I could listen to Peter and the Wolf again and again. Copland is one of my favourite composers of all time. His peculiar brass sounds are instantly recognizable. Billy the Kid is fantastic. I'm a big fan of Tchaikovsky. The Nutcracker Suite is a popular choice. I also have a lot of show tunes by Irving Berlin, Johnny Mercer, Lerner and Loewe, Harold Arlen, Rodgers and Hammerstein, and the legendary Holland-Dozier-Holland. I have a lot of respect for those guys.

I really enjoy Mexican food. As a vegetarian, fresh fruits and veggies are a favourite of mine.

I'm a sucker for toys and gadgets. I enjoy seeing what new products manufacturers have released. If there's something truly amazing, I'll buy it.

I'm obsessed with monkeys, especially chimps. Bubbles, my monkey, is a continual source of joy. I adore taking him on trips or excursions with me. He's an excellent pet and a great distraction.

Elizabeth Taylor is one of my favourite actresses. Her bravery inspires me. She's been through a lot and is a survivor. That lady has been through a lot and has managed to stand on her own two feet. Because of our shared experiences as child stars, I strongly identify with her. She told me she felt as if she had known me for years when we first started conversing on the phone. I had the same reaction.

Katharine Hepburn is another close buddy. At first, I was terrified about meeting her. We chatted briefly when I initially arrived on the set of On Golden Pond, where I was Jane Fonda's guest. She invited me to supper the following night. I felt quite fortunate. We've kept in touch and visited each other since then. Remember, it was Katharine Hepburn who convinced me to take off my sunglasses at the Grammys? She has had a significant impact on me. She, too, is a strong and private individual.

I feel that performers should strive to be strong role models for their audiences. It's amazing what a person can do if they just try. If you're under pressure, capitalise on it and utilise it to your advantage to improve whatever you're doing. Actors owe it to the public to be forceful and fair.

Historically, performers have frequently been sad figures. Many truly brilliant people have suffered or died as a result of stress and drugs, particularly liquor. It's heartbreaking. As a fan, you feel cheated since you didn't get to see them grow up. One can't help but wonder what Marilyn Monroe would have done or what Jimi Hendrix would have done in the 1980s.

Many celebrities have stated that they do not want their children to pursue careers in show business. I understand their emotions, but I disagree with them. "By all means, be my guest," I'd tell my son or daughter. Just walk right in. If you want to do it, go ahead and do it."

Nothing is more important to me than making others happy, relieving them of their concerns and worries, and helping to lighten their load. I want them to come away from one of my performances saying, "That was fantastic." I'd like to go back. "I had a fantastic time." That's what it's all about for me. That's fantastic. That's why I'm perplexed when celebrities declare they don't want their children in the show industry.

I believe people say this because they have been hurt. That makes sense to me. I've been there as well.

What one wishes for is to be touched by truth and to be able to interpret that truth so that one can use what one is feeling and experiencing, whether despair or joy, to add purpose to one's life and, ideally, to impact the lives of others.

This is the pinnacle of art. Those epiphanies are what I continue to strive for.

Printed in Great Britain
by Amazon